MICHAEL CARLBERG

Fiscal Policy Cyclical Budget Balance versus Fatal Crowding Out

Volkswirtschaftliche Schriften

Begründet von Prof. Dr. Dr. h. c. J. Broermann

Heft 401

Fiscal Policy

Cyclical Budget Balance versus Fatal Crowding Out

By

Michael Carlberg

Duncker & Humblot · Berlin

Gedruckt mit Unterstützung
der Universität der Bundeswehr Hamburg

CIP-Titelaufnahme der Deutschen Bibliothek

Carlberg, Michael:
Fiscal policy: cyclical budget balance versus fatal crowding out /
by Michael Carlberg. — Berlin: Duncker und Humblot, 1990
(Volkswirtschaftliche Schriften; H. 401)
ISBN 3-428-06942-0
NE: GT

Satz: Hagedornsatz, Berlin 46
Druck: Berliner Buchdruckerei Union GmbH, Berlin 61
Printed in Germany

ISSN 0505-9372
ISBN 3-428-06942-0

Over the business cycle as a whole, aim for budget surpluses.

Paul A. Samuelson
William D. Nordhaus

Preface

Fiscal policy is the instrument by means of which the government attempts to fight unemployment. Unfortunately, however, fiscal policy entails public debt, thus threatening to ruin the economy in the long run.

Strictly speaking, it will be argued that an investment shock generates a cyclical process of adjustment. This in turn requires a cyclical path of fiscal policy. In spite of that, the budget does not balance over the cycle as a whole. As a fundamental result, the long-run equilibrium proves to be unstable. Ultimately, the economy must break down. The theoretical analysis will be illustrated by making use of diagrams and numerical simulations.

I had many helpful talks with my colleagues at Hamburg: Hans Hermann Francke, Johannes Hackmann, Wolf Schäfer, Michael Schmid and Georg Tolkemitt. In addition, Romeo Grill, Harald Großmann, Jochen Michaelis and Daphni-Marina Papadopoulou carefully discussed with me all parts of the manuscript. Last but not least, Margarete Fritz typed the manuscript as excellently as ever. I would like to thank all of them.

Contents

1. Introduction

The present study is concerned with the short-run and long-run effects of fiscal policy on employment, output and prices. Suppose that an investment shock causes unemployment. Then it is the task of fiscal policy to restore full employment in the short run. This goes along with a budget deficit which adds to public debt. Here a number of questions arise: What are the long-run consequences of the fiscal expansion? Will public debt tend to explode? Will the stock of capital ultimately shrink back to zero? In other words, will there be fatal crowding out?

Fiscal policy induces various processes of adjustment which run at different speeds. This fact will be modelled here by distinguishing between the short-run equilibrium and the long long-run equilibrium. That is to say, in the short period only the fast variables accommodate, while in the long period the slow variables accommodate too. Properly speaking, in the short term money wages are rigid. The stock of capital and public debt are given exogenously. Technology is characterized by fixed coefficients since substitution is a slow process. In the long term, however, money wages are flexible. The stock of capital and public debt adapt themselves appropriately. The production function is smooth.

The analysis to be presented here starts from the seminal work done by Blinder and Solow (1973), Brunner and Meltzer (1976), Tobin and Buiter (1976) as well as Tobin (1986). Blinder and Solow (1973) reached the conclusion that the long-run effects of fiscal policy are even larger than the short-run effects. Brunner and Meltzer (1976) agreed that fiscal policy in the short period increases aggregate demand and hence output. In the long period, on the other hand, fiscal policy displaces private capital, thereby reducing output. As opposed to this, Tobin and Buiter (1976) insisted that the expansionary effect is permanent. Tobin (1986) investigated a lifecycle growth model, applying phase-diagram techniques. There the focus is on the long-run implications of the monetary-fiscal mix. Numerical simulations suggest that budget deficits may well end in catastrophes.

The basic exposition of the present monograph is as follows. To begin with, in chapters 2 and 3, we shall introduce the short-run equilibrium and the long-run equilibrium. Then, in chapter 4, the process of adjustment linking the short-run equilibrium and the long-run equilibrium will be sketched out briefly. What is more, in chapters 5 and 6, we shall argue that an investment shock generates a cyclical process of adjustment. This in turn requires a cyclical path of fiscal policy. As a result, the budget is balanced over the cycle. Finally, in chapter 7, the standard model will be extended in several directions.

For the remainder of the introduction, the approach to be taken will be set out in greater detail. At first, in chapter 2, we shall discuss the short-term impact of fiscal policy. The analysis will be carried out within the framework of an IS-LM model. Aggregate supply is perfectly elastic, so aggregate demand determines output.

Let us start with the goods market. The government purchases of goods and services are constant. In addition, the government levies a proportional tax on income. The budget deficit is defined as the excess of government purchases over tax revenue. Private consumption is an increasing function of disposable income, that is income net after tax. Private investment is a declining function of the rate of interest. Private consumption, private investment and government purchases sum up to aggregate demand. The goods market is in equilibrium, therefore output corresponds to aggregate demand.

Next we come to the money market. The central bank controls the nominal stock of money. The real demand for money is a declining function of the interest rate and an increasing function of income. The money market is in equilibrium, too, thus the real supply of money matches the real demand for money.

Now what are the short-run consequences of fiscal policy? Initially, there is full employment, and the budget is balanced. In this situation, an investment shock occurs. Sales expectations deteriorate, hence autonomous investment falls. Firms lower output and lay off workers, so unemployment develops. The reduction in income is accompanied by a reduction in tax proceeds, thus the budget gets into deficit. In order to reestablish full employment, the government buys more goods and services. As a response, firms raise output and engage additional workers. Moreover, the increase in government purchases enhances the budget deficit.

At this point we leave the short-run equilibrium and turn to the long-run equilibrium, see chapter 3. The investigation will be conducted within an overlapping generations model without bequests. This chapter offers the real analysis of a stationary economy.

Labour supply is assumed to be given exogenously. Money wages are flexible so as to clear the labour market. Put another way, full employment always prevails. In the long period, the production function is smooth. Output can be devoted to private consumption, private investment and public consumption. Firms maximize profits under perfect competition, therefore the interest rate equals the marginal product of capital. Analogously, the wage rate coincides with the marginal product of labour.

The government raises loans and collects an income tax to finance both public consumption and the interest payments on public debt. The government buys a constant amount of goods and services. Besides the government levies a proportional tax on factor income as well as on public interest. The budget deficit is composed of public consumption plus public interest minus tax receipts. It is covered by borrowing from the private sector. The budget deficit augments public debt.

The individual lifecycle consists of two periods, of the working period and of the retirement period. During the working period, the individual receives labour income, which he partly consumes and partly saves. The savings are used to buy government bonds and private bonds. During the retirement period, the individual earns interest on the bonds and sells the bonds altogether. The proceeds are entirely consumed, no bequests are left.

The utility of the representative individual depends on private consumption per head in the working period and on private consumption per head in the retirement period. The individual chooses present and future consumption so as to maximize utility subject to its budget constraint. The private savings of the active generation serve to finance public debt and private capital of the subsequent period.

The long-run equilibrium shows the following properties. Employment, the stock of capital and production are invariant. That means, firms do not invest. Output is completely consumed by households and by the government. Public debt does not change, so the budget is balanced.

Now what are the long-run consequences of fiscal policy? Imagine that the government increases public consumption, thereby contributing to the expansion of public debt. This displaces private capital, hence output comes down. The reduction in income causes a fall in private savings which further lowers the stock of capital and output. As capital becomes scarce, the rate of interest moves up. Together with the growth of public debt this raises public interest. In order to cover this, the government must borrow even more. It turns out that public debt will explode in the long term. This explosion drives capital down to zero. In other words, there will be fatal crowding out, thus eventually the economy must break down.

Here the question arises whether this vicious circle can be cured. Three possible answers will be examined more closely. First, the government restores public consumption to its initial value. Second, the government stabilizes public debt at the current level. And third, the government retires public debt completely.

In the short run, a fiscal expansion increases output. In the long run, however, output shrinks back to zero. Accordingly, in chapter 4, the process of adjustment linking the short-term equilibrium and the long-term equilibrium will be sketched out briefly. To begin with, in section 4.1., the supply side will be incorporated into the short-period analysis. Technology is characterized by fixed coefficients, since substitution is a slow process. The stock of capital and labour supply are given exogenously. Firms set the price equal to normal unit cost, which is the short-run expectation of unit costs.

In addition, actual output is restricted by the stock of capital and by labour supply. Capacity output is by definition that volume of output, at which the stock of capital is fully utilized. Full-employment output, analogously, is that volume of output at which all workers are engaged. So actual output is the minimum of aggregate demand, capacity output and full-employment output. Correspondingly, either a lack of aggregate demand, a capital shortage or a scarcity of workers may happen.

In the short period, money wages are downward rigid. Strictly speaking, when there is underemployment, money wages do not fall. Conversely, when there is overemployment, money wages rise so as to clear the labour market. A reduction in aggregate demand, starting from full employment, lowers output. This causes underemployment, yet money wages and prices do not react.

An increase in aggregate demand, on the other hand, raises output, thus creating overemployment. As a response, money wages take off. Firms mark up prices, thereby cutting down real balances. The interest rate is pushed up, which curbs private investment. Firms contract output and dismiss workers. This is the well-known Keynes effect. As a final result, output does not vary. There is still full employment, only prices have gone up.

Then, in section 4.2., we shall consider the medium-run equilibrium. Suppose that the government runs a budget deficit. This augments public debt round by round. The ensuing growth of public interest strengthens disposable income, consumption and aggregate demand. Moreover, in section 4.3., we shall broaden the long-run equilibrium. There, the real analysis of chapter 3 will be complemented by a monetary analysis.

Finally, in section 4.4., we shall have a look at the transition from short-period equilibrium to long-period equilibrium. At the outset, let the economy be in long-run equilibrium. In this situation suddenly an investment shock occurs. As a response, the government follows a policy of fiscal expansion. This sets in motion a drawn-out process of adjustment. The economy passes first through the short-run equilibrium and then through the medium-run equilibrium, ultimately settling down in the new long-run equilibrium.

In the short run, a loose fiscal policy improves output. But in the long run, it brings output down to zero. Judging from this, the long-term cost of fiscal policy seems to be forbidding. On the other hand, this raises the question whether the analysis done so far is really appropriate. Therefore, in chapters 5 and 6, it will be argued that an investment shock induces a cyclical process of adjustment. This in turn calls for a cyclical path of fiscal policy. As a fundamental result, the budget will be balanced over the cycle as a whole.

To begin with, in section 5.1., we shall regard an economy without public sector. The discussion will be carried out within an augmented multiplier-accelerator model of a stationary economy. Private consumption is a linear function of income. Private investment serves to close the gap between the desired and the actual stock of capital step by step. The desired stock of capital equals the capital-output ratio times expected sales. Expected sales are determined by the actual sales of the preceding period. Last but not least, private investment adds to the stock of capital.

In a sense, the process of adjustment divides into two phases. Initially, the economy is in the long-run equilibrium. All workers have got a job. Firms do not invest, so the stock of capital is constant. In the first phase, sales expectations worsen exogenously. For that reason, firms postpone the replacement of capital. Net investment becomes negative, hence the stock of capital declines. As a consequence, unemployment occurs.

In the second phase, sales expectations recover endogenously. On this ground, firms make good the replacement of capital. Net investment springs up, thus increasing the stock of capital. Accordingly, the economy suffers from overemployment. Will capital, employment and output finally return to their original values?

Then, in section 6.1., the public sector will enter the model. There the government pursues a passive fiscal policy. Public consumption is assumed to be fixed. The government imposes a proportional tax on both factor income and public interest. The budget deficit is defined by the excess of public consumption and public interest over tax revenue. The budget deficit leads to the accumulation of public debt.

Factor income and public interest, diminished by taxation, constitute disposable income. Private consumption is a linear function of disposable income. Private investment is used again to fill the gap between the desired and the actual stock of capital. The desired stock of capital depends on expected sales, which in turn are influenced by actual sales. The capital stock plus private investment this period give the capital stock next period.

In this case, too, the process of adjustment can be split up into two phases. At the start, the economy is in the steady state. The labour market clears. Firms abstain from investment, so the stock of capital is invariant. The budget is balanced, and no public debt does exist. Under these cirumstances, sales expectations deteriorate autonomously. This makes net investment negative and reduces the stock of capital. Consequently, unemployment emerges. The fall in income causes a fall in tax proceeds. The budget gets into deficit, thereby building up public debt round by round.

In the second phase, sales expectations improve again. This supports net investment and capital formation. The economy switches from underemployment to overemployment. The expansion of income brings in higher tax receipts. Now the government runs a budget surplus, put another way, the government redeems public debt. This involves two problems: Will public debt come home to zero or will it blow up? Will the capital stock regain its initial value or will it shrink back to zero?

Finally, in section 6.2., we shall postulate that the government follows an active fiscal policy. That means, public consumption is managed in such a way as to keep up full employment. Besides, the government levies a proportional tax on both factor income and public interest. Once more, the process of adjustment consists of two phases. At the beginning, the economy is in the stationary equilibrium. There is full employment. Firms do not invest, so the stock of capital does not move. The budget is balanced, and no public debt does exist.

In the first phase, sales expectations go down. As a response, firms defer the replacement of capital. In order to fight unemployment, the government immediately raises public consumption. The budget gets into deficit, thus starting the growth of public debt. In the second phase, sales expectations recover. For that reason, the replacement of capital is made up for. To prevent overemployment from coming into existence, the government lowers public consumption. The budget exhibits a surplus which cuts down public debt period by period. In the long run, however, public debt tends to explode. As a consequence, this drives capital down to zero. In other words, there will be fatal crowding out.

In summary, the investment shock generates a cyclical process of adjustment. What is needed, therefore, is a cyclical path of fiscal policy. In spite of this, the budget will not be balanced over the cycle. As a result, the long-run equilibrium proves to be unstable. Ultimately, the economy will collapse.

That is why we shall explore in section 6.2. if the government can maintain stability, too. There, the focus will be on two distinct strategies. First: Tax finance of public interest at full employment. And second: The government pays off the residual of public debt at full employment.

Last but not least, in chapter 7, the study will be extended to cover some more aspects. To begin with, in section 7.1., we shall take a look at the concept of full employment. The primary goal of fiscal policy is to restore full employment. How should this notion be defined within the framework of a cyclical model? Does full employment prevail at the ceiling of the process or at its average? Whether the budget can be balanced over the cycle or not depends heavily on the answer to this question.

Then, in section 7.2., emphasis will be laid on competing instruments to absorb an investment shock: money finance of budget deficits, investment subsidies and monetary policy. Next, in section 7.3., we shall leave the investment shock and turn to a monetary disturbance. At first the ensuing process of adjustment will be sketched out briefly. In addition we shall examine if fiscal or monetary policy are better suited to overcome the monetary disturbance.

So far the investigation concentrated on a stationary economy. Now, in section 7.4., we shall address a growing economy. In a stationary economy, a tax cut gives rise to fatal crowding out. Does this hold in a growing economy, too?

Moreover, the optimum of fiscal policy will be derived. In a stationary economy, the budget should be balanced across the cycle. In a growing economy, on the other hand, should the government run a budget deficit or a budget surplus over the cycle as a whole?

2. Short-Run Equilibrium

The present section deals with the short-term effects of fiscal policy. The analysis will be implemented within an IS-LM model of a closed economy. Aggregate supply is perfectly elastic, so output is determined by aggregate demand.

Let us begin with the goods market. The government buys a given amount of goods and services $G=\text{const}$. Besides, the government levies a tax $T=tY$ at the flat rate $t=\text{const}$ on income Y. Disposable income is defined as income net after tax $Y_d=Y-T$. Private consumption is an increasing function of disposable income $C=C(Y_d)$ with $0<C_1<1$. Here $C_1=dC/dY_d$ denotes the marginal propensity to consume. Taking account of $Y_d=(1-t)Y$, the consumption function can be restated as $C=C[(1-t)Y]$. Private investment is a declining function $I=I(i)$ of the rate of interest i with $I_1<0$. Private consumption, private investment and government purchases sum up to aggregate demand $Z=C+I+G$. The goods market is in equilibrium, hence output Y equals aggregate demand $Y=C+I+G$ or:

(1) $$Y=C[(1-t)Y]+I(i)+G$$

Next have a look at the money market.The central bank fixes the nominal stock of money $M=\text{const}$. The real demand for money is a declining function of the interest rate and an increasing function of income $L=L(i, Y)$ with $L_1<0$ and $L_2>0$. The money market is in equilibrium too, that is, real balances coincide with the real demand for money $M/P=L$, where P symbolizes the price level. Accordingly:

(2) $$\frac{M}{P}=L(i, Y)$$

As a consequence, the short-run equilibrium can be characterized by a system of two equations (1) and (2).

Figure 1 visualizes the short-run equilibrium. The downward sloping IS curve shows all combinations of income and interest rate which clear the goods market, compare equation (1). Analogously, the upward sloping LM curve indicates all pairs of income and interest rate which equilibrate the money market, see equation (2). The point of intersection marks the simultaneous equilibrium of both markets, thus Y_o is the equilibrium income. An autonomous reduction in private investment shifts the IS curve to the left. Conversely, an increase in government purchases moves the IS curve to the right. And a monetary expansion pushes the LM curve rightward.

We come now to the government budget. When government purchases exceed tax revenue $G>T$, the government runs a budget deficit. By the same token, when government purchases fall short of tax revenue $G<T$, the budget is in surplus. Strictly speaking, the budget deficit is defined as the excess of government purchases over tax revenue $B=G-T$ or

(3) $$B=G-tY$$

The budget is balanced $B=0$, if government purchases exactly match tax revenue $G=T$. From $tY=G$ follows

(4) $$Y_B=\frac{G}{t}$$

Y_B stands for the level of income at which the budget is in equilibrium. The vertical GT line in Figure 1 represents the balanced budget line. In the case depicted there the budget exhibits a deficit. And an autonomous increase in government purchases shifts the GT line to the right.

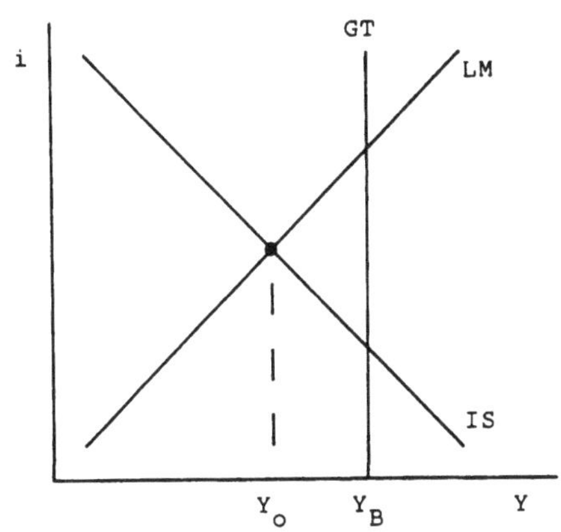

Figure 1. Short-Run Equilibrium and Balanced Budget Line.

In addition, $\bar{Y}$ will be that volume of output at which all workers have got a job. Figure 2 reveals the vertical full-employment line in the IS-LM diagram. In the situation given there, the economy suffers from unemployment.

Having laid this groundwork, we return to the initial problem: What is the short-term impact of fiscal policy? At the start, let there be full employment, and let the budget be balanced. In figure 3, the full equilibrium can be found in the common point of intersection of the IS curve, the LM curve, the GT line and the $\bar{Y}$ vertical. Now suppose that an investment shock occurs. Sales expectations worsen exogenously, thereby lowering autonomous investment. In figure 3, the IS curve moves to the left. As a consequence, unemployment arises, and the budget gets into deficit. In order to restore full employment, the government buys more goods and services. In the diagram, the IS curve is pushed back in its initial position. What is more, the GT curve goes to the right, signalling that the fiscal expansion increases the budget deficit even further.

To illustrate this, consider a numerical example with linear relationships of behaviour:

(5) $$C = \bar{C} + c(1-t)Y$$

(6) $$I = \bar{I} - bi$$

(7) $$L = kY - hi$$

(5) is the consumption function, (6) the investment function and (7) the money demand function. The parameters of the model assume the following values: autonomous consumption $\bar{C}=0$, marginal propensity to consume $c=0.8$, tax rate $t=0.25$, autonomous investment $\bar{I}=825$, interest sensitivity of investment $b=50$, government purchases $G=875$, income sensitivity of money demand $k=0.25$, interest sensitivity of money demand $h=62.5$, real quantity of money $M/P=500$.

Now solve the model for Y to obtain the equilibrium income of $Y=3500$. We postulate that at this level of output all workers are engaged. The rate of interest amounts to $i=6$. The government receives $T=875$ in taxes, so the budget is balanced. Against this background, sales expectations deteriorate, say autonomous investment drops from 825 to 525. This shock depresses output to 3000 and in this way creates unemployment. The rate of interest is cut down to 4 percent. The diminution in income is accompanied by a diminution in tax proceeds to 750, so the budget gets into a deficit of 125. To lift output again to the full-employment level of 3500, the government steps up its purchases from 875 to 1175. The rate of interest climbs back to 6 percent. The rise in income brings in more taxes $T=875$. But the increase in government purchases dominates, thus the budget deficit swells to 300.

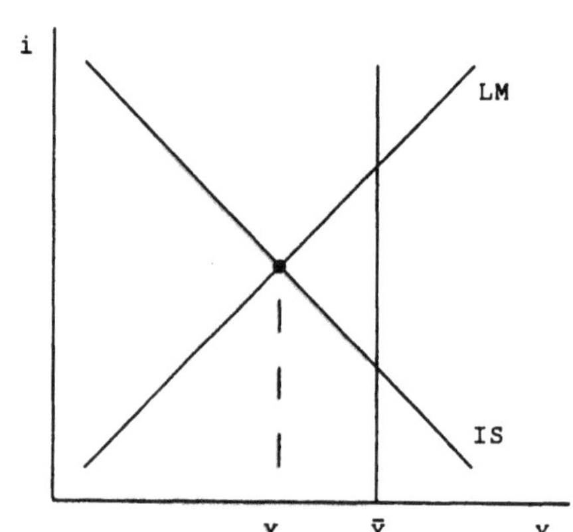

Figure 2. Short-Run Equilibrium and Full-Employment Line.

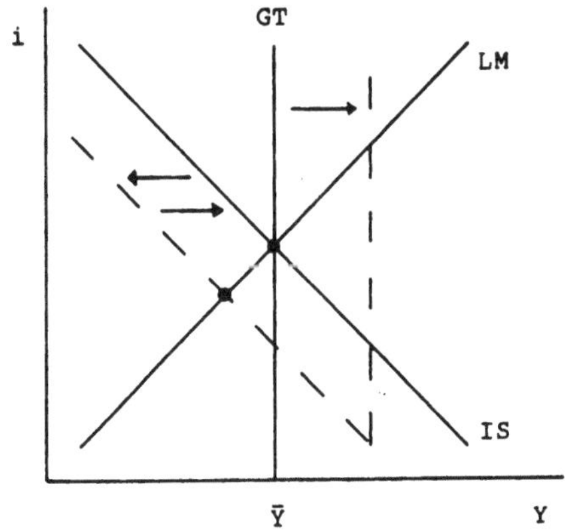

Figure 3. Investment Shock and Fiscal Policy.

Table 1 provides a synopsis of the adjustment process. Initially, the economy is in full equilibrium, see column 1. The labor market clears, and the budget is balanced. Then the investment shock causes both unemployment and a budget deficit, compare column 2. The government reacts by a fiscal expansion. First of all, this measure guarantees full employment, confer column 3. On the other hand, it enhances the budget deficit once more.

Table 1
Investment Shock and Fiscal Policy

	1	2	3
$\bar{I}$	825	525	525
G	875	875	1175
Y	3500	3000	3500
i	6	4	6
T	875	750	875
B	0	125	300

3. Long-Run Equilibrium

In the current chapter, we shall discuss the long-term effects of fiscal policy. To begin with, in section 3.1., we shall introduce the long-period equilibrium. There, the focus will be on the existence of a steady state. Then, in section 3.2., we shall keep track of the process of adjustment. In that place, emphasis will be laid on the stability of equilibrium. To illustrate this, in section 3.3., we shall perform a numerical simulation of the time path. Finally, in section 3.4., public consumption will enter the utility function explicitly.

3.1. Long-Run Equilibrium

The investigation will be conducted within an overlapping generations model without bequests (Diamond 1965). This chapter offers a real analysis of a stationary economy. Labour supply is assumed to be given exogenously $\bar{N}$ = const. In the long run, wages are flexible so as to adapt labour demand N to labour supply $\bar{N}$:

(1) $$N = \bar{N}$$

Put differently, full employment prevails forever.

Firms produce a homogeneous commodity Y by means of capital K and labour N. Properly speaking, N denotes the number of active workers. For ease of exposition, consider a Cobb-Douglas technology showing constant returns to scale:

(2) $$Y = K^{\alpha} N^{\beta}$$

with $\alpha > 0$, $\beta > 0$ and $\alpha + \beta = 1$. Output Y can be devoted to private consumption C, private investment I and public consumption G:

(3) $$Y = C + I + G$$

Firms maximize profits ¶ under perfect competition:

(4) $$¶ = Y - iK - wN$$

where w symbolizes the wage rate. Differentiate (4) for K, set the derivative equal to zero and rearrange:

(5) $$i = \frac{\partial Y}{\partial K} = \frac{\alpha Y}{K}$$

That means, the interest rate corresponds to the marginal product of capital. Analogously, the wage rate coincides with the marginal product of labour:

(6) $$w=\frac{\partial Y}{\partial N}=\frac{\beta Y}{N}$$

The government raises loans and imposes an income tax to finance both public consumption and the interest payments on public debt. The government buys a specified volume of goods and services $G=\text{const}$. D stands for public debt owed by the government to the private sector. The government pays the interest rate i on public debt D, so public interest equals iD. The government collects a proportional tax T on factor income Y and on public interest $T=t(Y+iD)$ with $t=\text{const}$.

Here, the budget deficit B is defined as the excess of public consumption and public interest over tax receipts $B=G+iD-T$ or:

(7) $$B=G+iD-t(Y+iD)$$

The government covers the budget deficit by borrowing from the private sector. Equation (7) is commonly called the government budget constraint. In the short-run equilibrium, public interest was implicitly assumed to be zero $iD=0$, see chapter 2. Public debt this period D plus public borrowing this period B gives public debt next period D_{+1}:

(8) $$D_{+1}=D+B$$

In the long-run equilibrium, public debt does not change $D_{+1}=D$, hence the budget is balanced:

(9) $$B=0$$

Taking account of this, (7) can be reformulated as:

(10) $$G+iD=t(Y+iD)$$

The individual lifecycle is composed of two periods, of the working period and of the retirement period. During the working period, the individual receives labour income, which he partly consumes and partly saves. The savings are used to buy government bonds and private bonds. During the retirement period, the individual earns interest on the bonds and sells the bonds altogether. The proceeds are entirely consumed, no bequests are left.

The utility u of the representative individual depends on private consumption per head in the working period c^1 and on private consumption per head in the retirement period c^2. Take a logarithmic utility function:

(11) $$u=\gamma \log c^1+\delta \log c^2$$

with $\gamma>0$, $\delta>0$ and $\eta+\delta=1$.

The budget constraint of the representative individual covers the whole lifecycle. $(1-t)w$ is net labour income in the working period and $(1-t)w-c^1$ are private savings in the working period. The individual earns the net rate of interest $(1-t)i$ on private savings, so private consumption in the retirement period is $[(1-t)w-c^1]\,[1+(1-t)i]=c^2$. As a consequence, the individual budget constraint can be stated as:

$$c^1+\frac{c^2}{1+(1-t)i}=(1-t)w \tag{12}$$

The individual chooses present and future consumption so as to maximize utility subject to its budget constraint. The evaluation of the Lagrange function yields private consumption per head in the working period:

$$c^1=\gamma(1-t)w \tag{13}$$

Net labour income minus private consumption per head gives private savings per head $s=(1-t)w-c^1$ or

$$s=\delta(1-t)w \tag{14}$$

The private savings of the active generation amount to $S=sN$. Observe (14) and (6) to arrive at:

$$S=\beta\delta(1-t)Y \tag{15}$$

The private savings of the young generation serve to finance public debt and private capital of the subsequent period:

$$D_{+1}+K_{+1}=S \tag{16}$$

In the long-run equilibrium, both public debt and the capital stock are invariant $D_{+1}=D$ and $K_{+1}=K$. Insert this together with (15) into (16) to reach:

$$D+K=\beta\delta(1-t)Y \tag{17}$$

Besides, private investment augments the stock of capital:

$$K_{+1}=K+I \tag{18}$$

In the steady state, the stock of capital is uniform, so firms do not invest:

$$I=0 \tag{19}$$

In summary, the long-run equilibrium can be described by a system of four equations:

$$Y=K^{\alpha}N^{\beta} \tag{20}$$

$$i=\alpha Y/K \tag{21}$$

$$D+K=\beta\delta(1-t)Y \tag{22}$$

$$G+iD=t(Y+iD) \tag{23}$$

$\alpha, \beta, \delta, t, G$ and N are given exogenously, whereas i, D, K and Y are endogenous variables. There are as many equations as unknowns, hence the solution is determinate.

As a result, the long-run equilibrium shows the following properties. There is full employment. Labour supply, the stock of capital and output are constant. Firms do not invest. Output is completely consumed by households and by the government. Public debt does not change, so the budget is balanced. In other words, this is a stationary economy.

Having laid this groundwork, we return to the initial problem: What are the long-run effects of fiscal policy? At the beginning, let the economy be in the steady state. Without losing generality, we postulate that there is no public debt $D=0$. In this situation, the government increases public consumption, while leaving the tax rate fixed. The key question is: What are the attributes of the new long-run equilibrium?

The steady state without public debt can be represented in the following way:

(24) $$Y=K^{\alpha} N^{\beta}$$

(25) $$i=\alpha Y/K$$

(26) $$K=\beta\delta(1-t)Y$$

(27) $$G=tY$$

Here the tax rate becomes endogenous. The number of equations matches the number of unknowns (i, t, K, Y), thus the system can be solved.

Now take the total differentials of the original system (20) to (23) at the point $D=0$:

(28) $$dY=\alpha K^{\alpha-1} N^{\beta} dK$$

(29) $$i=\alpha K^{\alpha-1} N^{\beta}$$

(30) $$dD+dK=\beta\delta(1-t)\,dY$$

(31) $$dG+i\,dD=t\,dY+it\,dD$$

The comparison of (28) and (29) reveals $dY=i\,dK$. Next we derive the interest rate which holds in the initial equilibrium. Substitute (26) into $i=\alpha Y/K$ to obtain:

(32) $$i=\frac{\alpha}{\beta\delta(1-t)}$$

Eliminate i in $dY=i\,dK$ with the help of (32) and rearrange:

(33) $$dK=\frac{\beta\delta(1-t)}{\alpha}dY$$

Then put this into (30) and multiply by $\alpha/[\beta\delta(1-t)]$:

(34) $$dY = -\frac{\alpha}{\beta^2\,\delta(1-t)}\,dD$$

According to (34), a rise in public debt leads to a fall in output. Further, combine (31) with (32) and (34) to get:

(35) $$dG = -\left[\frac{\alpha}{\beta\delta} + \frac{\alpha t}{\beta^2\,\delta(1-t)}\right]dD$$

The term in brackets is positive. As a consequence, a rise in public consumption causes a fall in public debt.

This outcome can be interpreted in the following way. Imagine that the government increases public consumption. The loose fiscal policy lowers public debt, thereby raising the stock of capital and output. At first sight, this seems to be somewhat like a paradox. Remember that at the start no public debt existed. Therefore, due to the fiscal expansion, public debt becomes negative. That implies, the government in the past has made loans to the private sector. Now it receives interest payments in exchange. Here the question arises whether the process of adjustment will actually lead to the new steady state. As a result, a long-run equilibrium does indeed exist. But one might suspect that it will prove to be unstable.

So far we studied an increase in public consumption. Instead we shall now examine a reduction in the tax rate. Initially, the economy is in the steady state, and there is no public debt $D=0$. Under these circumstances, the government lowers the tax rate, leaving public consumption unaffected. What are the comparative statics of this action?

Again the system from (24) until (27) provides the long-run equilibrium without public debt. At first take the total differentials of the original system (20) to (23) in the place $D=0$:

(36) $$dY = \alpha\,K^{\alpha-1}\,N^{\beta}\,dK$$

(37) $$i = \alpha\,K^{\alpha-1}\,N^{\beta}$$

(38) $$dD + dK = \beta\delta\,dY - \beta\delta\,Y\,dt - \beta\delta t\,dY$$

(39) $$i\,dD = Y\,dt + t\,dY + it\,dD$$

What we are interested in is to express dD as a function of dt. For that purpose insert (37) into (36), thereby reaching $dY = i\,dK$. Then eliminate dK in (38) by means of $dY = i\,dK$ and reshuffle terms:

(40) $$\beta\delta i Y\,dt + i\,dD = [\beta\delta i(1-t) - 1]\,dY$$

In the next step we want to get rid of dY in (40). On this account solve (39) for dY:

$$dY=\frac{i(1-t)}{t}dD-\frac{Y}{t}dt \tag{41}$$

Finally substitute (41) into (40) and rearrange adequately:

$$dD=\frac{Y-\beta\delta iY}{i-\beta\delta\, i^2\,(1-t)^2}dt \tag{42}$$

Now what is the sign of the multiplier in (42)? The initial rate of interest is still given by (32). It is convenient to rewrite this formula as:

$$1-\beta\delta i=\frac{1-t-\alpha}{1-t} \tag{43}$$

From the empirical point of view, it is sound to assume that $1-t-\alpha$ is positive. Under this condition, the numerator in (42) is also positive. Further (32) can be transformed into $\beta\delta i(1-t)=\alpha$ or:

$$1-\beta\delta i(1-t)^2=1-\alpha(1-t) \tag{44}$$

As a rule, analogously, (44) is positive. Hence the denominator in (42) is positive, too. From this follows that the multiplier in (42) is positive as well. As a consequence, a fall in the tax rate induces a fall in public debt. Finally have a look at (40) where the term in brackets ist negative. Accordingly, the tax cut and the accompanying decumulation of public debt raise output and thus capital.

In summary, imagine that the government reduces the tax rate. It has been demonstrated above that the fiscal expansion lowers public debt, whereas both the stock of capital and output go up. This effect seems to be a bit paradoxical. Strictly speaking, the tax cut gives rise to negative public debt, since at the start public debt amounted to zero. The government has lent money to the private sector and now gets interest payments on public assets. Will there be a trajectory linking the old and the new long-run equilibrium?

As a result, a steady state does indeed exist. On the other hand, one may doubt that it will turn out to be stable. Essentially, this confirms the conclusions drawn for the increase in public consumption.

3.2. Process of Adjustment

In the current section, we shall explore the stability of the long-run equilibrium. First of all, consider an increase in public consumption. At the beginning, in period 0, let the economy be in the steady state. Without loss of generality, there is no public debt $D=0$, and the budget is balanced $G=tY$.

Against this background, in period 1, the government raises public consumption, while the tax rate remains constant. The stock of capital has been determined in period 0, so income and private savings of the young do not change $K_1 = K_0$, $Y_1 = Y_0$ and $S_1 = S_0$. The rise in public consumption $G_1 > G_0$ brings the budget into deficit, hence public debt builds up $D_2 = G_1 - t\,Y_1 > 0$. A good deal of private wealth is absorbed by public debt, the residual being left for private capital $K_2 = S_1 - D_2$. As a corollary, the stock of capital declines $K_2 < K_1$.

At this point we enter period 2. The reduction in the stock of capital gives rise to a reduction in output and in private savings $Y_2 < Y_1$ and $S_2 < S_1$. Now the government must pay interest on public debt, therefore the budget deficit amounts to:

(1) $$D_3 - D_2 = G_2 - t\,Y_2 + i_2(1-t)D_2$$

From $G_2 > G_0$ and $Y_2 < Y_0$ one can deduce that $G_2 > t\,Y_2$. Of course, net public interest is positive $i_2(1-t)D_2 > 0$. Thus (1) in fact is positive. In other words, public debt continues to accumulate. Private wealth serves to finance public debt and private capital $K_3 = S_2 - D_3$. Correspondingly, the increment in the stock of capital equals:

(2) $$K_3 - K_2 = (S_2 - S_1) - (D_3 - D_2)$$

$K_3 - K_2$ is negative because of $S_2 - S_1 < 0$. Put another way, the stock of capital keeps on shrinking. Obviously, this process repeats itself round by round.

To sum up, the increase in public consumption raises public debt, thereby lowering both the stock of capital and output. These dynamics are in sharp constrast to the comparative statics discussed above. There the increase in public consumption reduced public debt, while the stock of capital and output moved up. As a major consequence, the steady state proves to be unstable. In the long run, public debt tends to explode. This explosion in turn drives the stock of capital and output down to zero. That is to say, there will be fatal crowding out, and ultimately the economy will break down.

One might object here that the production function was assumed to be of the Cobb-Douglas type. Yet this assumption was made for ease of exposition only. The correct answer would be: Even under a well-behaved Cobb-Douglas technology, the loose fiscal policy cannot be sustained.

So far emphasis was laid on an increase in public consumption. Now the focus will shift to a reduction in the tax rate. Apart from this, we take the same approach as before. Initially, in period 0, the economy is in the stationary state. No public debt does exist $D = 0$, and the budget is in equilibrium $G = t\,Y$.

Under these circumstances, in period 1, the government lowers the tax rate, whereas public consumption stays put. Again, the stock of capital has been fixed in period 0, hence output does not vary $K_1 = K_0$ and $Y_1 = Y_0$. Owing to $t_1 < t_0$ and $S = \beta\delta(1-t)\,Y$, we arrive at $S_1 > S_0$. The tax cut creates a budget deficit, so public debt comes into existence $D_2 = G - t_1\,Y_1 > 0$. The portfolio is composed of public debt and private capital $K_2 = S_1 - D_2$. Accordingly, the change in private capital can be written as:

(3) $$K_2 - K_1 = (S_1 - S_0) - (D_2 - D_1) = \beta\delta(1 - t_1) Y_1 - \beta\delta(1 - t_0) Y_0 - G + t_1 Y_1$$

Next insert $G = t_0 Y_0$ as well as $Y_1 = Y_0$ and collect terms:

(4) $$K_2 - K_1 = (1 - \beta\delta)(t_1 - t_0) Y_0 < 0$$

That means, the stock of capital declines.

At this juncture, we close period 1 and open up period 2. The drop in capital leads to a drop in income and private savings $Y_2 < Y_1$ and $S_2 < S_1$. Here the budget deficit also comprises net public interest:

(5) $$D_3 - D_2 = G - t_2 Y_2 + i_2 (1 - t_2) D_2$$

$t_2 < t_0$ and $Y_2 < Y_0$ imply that $G > t_2 Y_2$. As a matter of fact, net public interest is positive $i_2 (1 - t_2) D_2 > 0$. Thus public debt continues to grow. What is more, a certain proportion of private wealth is diverted by public debt, the remainder being left for private capital $K_3 = S_2 - D_3$. Therefore, the variation in the stock of capital is:

(6) $$K_3 - K_2 = (S_2 - S_1) - (D_3 - D_2)$$

As a consequence, the stock of capital keeps on shrinking. The economy ends up in a vicious circle where the government borrows in order to finance the interest payments on public debt.

To conclude, the reduction in the tax rate enhances public debt, thereby depressing the stock of capital and output. Evidently, this process does not converge to the new long-run equilibrium. In the new steady, public debt is lower, while the stock of capital and output are higher. Put another way, the stationary equilibrium turns out to be unstable. In the long run, public debt tends to blow up, which squeezes capital and output to zero. There will be fatal crowding out, so eventually the economy will collapse. These findings underline the importance of the results obtained for the increase in public consumption.

Here the question arises whether the government can stop this vicious circle. Three potential solutions will be investigated in greater detail. First, the government lifts the tax rate back to its initial value. Second, the government stabilizes public debt at the current level. Properly speaking, the government varies the tax rate so as to keep public debt constant. And third, the government retires public debt altogether. More precisely, the government sets t such that $D = 0$.

To begin with, suppose that the government raises the tax rate to its original value. The increment in public debt amounts to

(7) $$D_{+1} - D = G - tY + i(1 - t)D$$

as is well known. By virtue of $G > tY$ and $i(1-t)D > 0$ it can be established that (7) is positive. In other words, public debt continues to surge. Analogously, the addition to the stock of capital equals:

$$K_{+1} - K = (S - S_{-1}) - (D_{+1} - D) \tag{8}$$

With respect to $S = \beta\delta(1-t)Y$, one can say that t goes up while Y comes down, thus diminishing private wealth. From this follows that (8) ist negative, so the stock of capital (and output) keeps on falling. This process recurs period by period. The stock of capital and output shrink back to zero, hence finally the economy breaks down.

Next it will be assumed that the government stabilizes public debt at the current level. Strictly speaking, the government adapts the tax rate so as to hold public debt fast:

$$D_{+1} - D = G + iD - t(Y + iD) = 0 \tag{9}$$

Now solve the right-hand side of (9) for t to get the required rate of taxation:

$$t = \frac{G + iD}{Y + iD} \tag{10}$$

Apparently, the government must boost the tax rate even more. Once again, the change in the stock of capital is given by:

$$K_{+1} - K = (S - S_{-1}) - (D_{+1} - D) \tag{11}$$

As far as $S = \beta\delta(1-t)Y$ is concerned, t is pushed up, whereas Y is pulled down. For that reason, private savings dwindle. As a consequence, (11) ist negative. That is to say, the stock of capital (and output) continues to decline. This vicious circle reproduces itself round by round, driving the stock of capital and output down to zero. Unfortunately, the economy suffers from fatal crowding out.

The third point refers to the redemption of public debt. More exactly, we posit that the government sets the tax rate so as to pay off public debt completely. Under the condition $D_{+1} = 0$, the budget constraint simplifies to:

$$D + G + iD = t(Y + iD) \tag{12}$$

In the current period, the government raises the tax rate substantially in order to finance public debt, public consumption and public interest. (12) yields the tax rate which is needed to do this job:

$$t = \frac{D + G + iD}{Y + iD} \tag{13}$$

Hence the analysis reduces to an overlapping generations model without public debt. This model is well known to be stable, so eventually the economy returns to its original equilibrium. No problem will be left.

At this stage, we shall switch over from loose to tight fiscal policy. That is to say, the government increases the tax rate. At the start, in period 0, the economy is in the steady state. There is no public debt $D=0$, and the budget is balanced $G=tY$.

In this situation, in period 1, the government raises the tax rate, while public consumption remains unchanged. The stock of capital has been decided on in period 0, thus output is invariant $K_1=K_0$ and $Y_1=Y_0$. The evaluation of $S=\beta\delta(1-t)Y$ shows that private savings diminish $S_1<S_0$. The tax rise moves the budget into surplus, consequently negative public debt occurs $D_2=G-t_1 Y_1<0$. From this one can infer that $D_2<D_1$. Private wealth and public wealth serve to cover private capital $K_2=S_1-D_2$. Accordingly, the increment in the stock of capital amounts to:

$$K_2-K_1=(S_1-S_0)-(D_2-D_1)= \beta\delta(1-t_1)Y_1-\beta\delta(1-t_0)Y_0-G+t_1 Y_1 \tag{14}$$

Then note $G=t_0 Y_0$ as well as $Y_1=Y_0$ and collect terms:

$$K_2-K_1=(1-\beta\delta)(t_1-t_0)Y_0 \tag{15}$$

(15) is positive since $t_1>t_0$. As a consequence, capital accumulates.

Here we enter period 2. The increase in capital induces an increase in output and private savings $Y_2>Y_1$ and $S_2>S_1$. Now the government receives interest payments on public assets:

$$D_3-D_2=G-t_2 Y_2+i_2(1-t_2)D_2 \tag{16}$$

$t_2>t_0$ and $Y_2>Y_0$ involve $G<t_2 Y_2$. Moreover, net public interest is negative $i_2(1-t_2)D_2<0$. Therefore, (16) is also negative. In other words, public assets continue to build up. Due to $K_3=S_2-D_3$, the variation in the stock of capital equals:

$$K_3-K_2=(S_2-S_1)-(D_3-D_2) \tag{17}$$

(17) is positive, as can be seen from $S_2-S_1>0$ and $D_3-D_2<0$. Put differently, the stock of capital keeps on growing.

As a result, the tax increase reduces public debt, thereby raising the stock of capital and output. Once again, the dynamics is not consistent with the comparative statics. In the new long-run equilibrium, public debt is higher, whereas capital and output are lower. Evidently, the steady state proves to be unstable. The fiscal contraction ultimately pushes public debt to minus infinity. The stock of capital and output, however, tend to explode.

Finally we shall give an overview of the present section. An increase in public consumption drives capital down to zero, hence the economy will break down. A reduction in the tax rate leads to fatal crowding out, too. Can the government cure this process? When the government lifts the tax rate back to its initial value, then nevertheless the economy will collapse. The same holds true when the government tries to stabilize public debt at its current level. There seems to be no easy way out. The government can stop the vicious circle only by retiring public debt altogether.

Public debt is so to speak like a killer virus. It breeds itself and displaces all other activities.

3.3. Simulation

To illustrate the long-run equilibrium and the process of adjustment, we shall perform some numerical computations. Let us begin with the comparative statics. Initially, the economy is in the steady state. No public debt does exist $D=0$. Now, suddenly, the equilibrium becomes disturbed. The government reduces the tax rate, leaving public consumption unaffected. Then, what does the new steady state look like? To answer this question, regard a numerical example with $\alpha=0.3$, $\beta=0.7$, $\gamma=0.6$, $\delta=0.4$, $t=0.2$ and $N=100$.

The stationary equilibrium without public debt can be described by a system of three equations:

(1) $$Y=K^{\alpha} N^{\beta}$$

(2) $$K=\beta\delta(1-t)Y$$

(3) $$G=tY$$

Here α, β, δ, t and N are given exogenously, whereas G, K and Y are endogenous variables. There are as many equations as unknowns, so the system is definite. First substitute (1) into (2) and solve for $K=[\beta\delta(1-t)]^{1/\beta} N$. Then insert the numerical parameters of the model on the right-hand side to arrive at $K=11.80$, $Y=52.67$, $T=10.53$ and $G=10.53$. Now imagine that the government lowers the tax rate from $t=0.2$ to $t=0.1$. What will be the effect of this measure on the long-run equilibrium?

The steady state with public debt can be characterized by a system of four equations, as is familiar from section 3.1.:

(4) $$Y=K^{\alpha} N^{\beta}$$

(5) $$i=\alpha Y/K$$

(6) $$D+K=\beta\delta(1-t)Y$$

(7) $$G+iD=t(Y+iD)$$

In this case, t, G and N are given exogenously, while i, D, K and Y are endogenous variables. The number of equations matches the number of unknowns, so the solution is determinate.

After putting the parameter values into (4) until (7), the system takes on the shape:

(8) $$Y=25.12\,K^{0.3}$$

(9) $$i = 0.3\ Y/K$$

(10) $$D + K = 0.252\ Y$$

(11) $$10.53 + 0.9\ iD = 0.1\ Y$$

To solve this system, eliminate Y in (9) by means of (8):

(12) $$i = 7.536\ K^{-0.7}$$

Further, insert (8) into (10) and rearrange:

(13) $$D = 6.330\ K^{0.3} - K$$

Moreover, multiply (12) by (13) to obtain public interest:

(14) $$iD = 47.70\ K^{-0.4} - 7.536\ K^{0.3}$$

Finally, combine (11) with (8) and (14):

(15) $$10.53 + 42.93\ K^{-0.4} = 9.294\ K^{0.3}$$

The analysis of (15) yields the equilibrium value of the stock of capital $K = 21.1$. From this one can infer immediately $Y = 62.7$ and $D = -5.3$. The rate of interest amounts to 0.891, so public interest reaches $iD = -4.722$. This can be verified by checking that the budget will be balanced.

So far, we considered a tax cut. Instead, we shall now explore a tax increase. At the outset, again, the economy is in the steady state, and there is no public debt. Under these circumstances, the government raises the tax rate from $t = 0.2$ to $t = 0.3$, thereby disrupting the long-run equilibrium. What will be the salient features of the new steady state? In full analogy to (15), one can deduce that $10.53 + 33.39\ K^{-0.4} = 12.81\ K^{0.3}$. The numerical evaluation provides $K = 8.7$, $Y = 48.1$ and $D = 3.4$. The rate of interest equals 1.659, hence public interest is $iD = 5.64$.

Table 2 presents a survey of the numerical simulation. Initially, the economy is in the stationary equilibrium, compare column 1. Firms manufacture 52.7 units by making use of 11.8 machines and 100 workers. Against this background, the government reduces the tax rate from 0.2 to 0.1, see column 2. As a response, public debt falls from 0 to -5.3, but capital rises from 11.8 to 21.1. In other words, the government becomes a creditor, thus stimulating capital formation. Conversely, suppose that the government increases the tax rate from 0.2 to 0.3, confer column 3. This action raises public debt from 0 to 3.4., whilst lowering capital from 11.8 to 8.7. That is to say, the government becomes a debtor, who crowds out private capital.

According to figure 1, public debt is an increasing function of the tax rate. The stock of capital, on the other hand, is a declining function of the tax rate.

At this point, we leave the comparative statics and turn to the dynamics. Once more, the computations are based on the following parameter values: $\alpha = 0.3$, $\beta = 0.7$, $\gamma = 0.6$, $\delta = 0.4$, $t = 0.2$ and $N = 100$. To begin with, have a look at a tax

Table 2
Tax Rate and Capital Stock (Comparative Statics)

t	0.2	0.1	0.3
K	11.8	21.1	8.7
N	100	100	100
Y	52.7	62.7	48.1
G	10.5	10.5	10.5
D	0	- 5.3	3.4
i	1.34	0.89	1.66
iD	0	- 4.7	5.6
T	10.5	5.8	16.1
B	0	0	0

cut. At the start, the economy is in the steady state, and no public debt does exist. Now assume that the government reduces the tax rate, which sets in motion a drawn-out process of adjustment.

Properly speaking, in period 0, the economy is in the long-run equilibrium at a tax rate of $t=0.2$. As is well known from the comparative statics, the stock of capital amounts to $K=11.80$, so firms produce $Y=52.67$. Owing to $S=\beta\delta(1-t)Y$, private savings of the young generation equal $S=11.80$. Further, public consumption agrees with tax revenue $G=tY=10.53$. There is no public debt $D=0$. Private assets this period give the stock of capital next period $K_{+1}=S$.

In this situation, in period 1, the government lowers the tax rate to $t=0.1$. The stock of capital has been determined in period 0, hence the tax cut does not affect output for the moment $K=11.80$ and $Y=52.67$. The tax cut actually increases private savings $S=\beta\delta(1-t)Y=13.27$. Besides, the tax cut creates a budget deficit, which adds to public debt $D_{+1}=G-tY=5.26$. A good deal of private assets is absorbed by public debt, the remainder being left for private capital $K_{+1}=S-D_{+1}=8.01$. Public debt rises by more than private assets, which contributes to a fall in private capital.

At this juncture, we enter period 2.The diminution in the stock of capital leads to a diminution in output and income $Y=46.89$. Therefore, private savings come down once more $S=\beta\delta(1-t)Y=11.82$. The rate of interest corresponds to the marginal product of capital $i=1.76$, so public interest amounts to

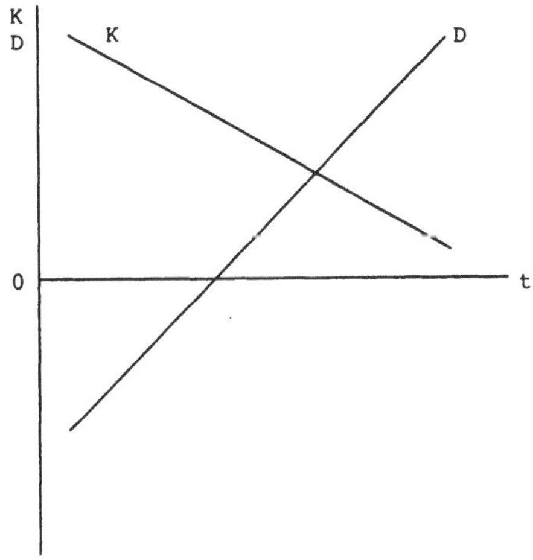

Figure 1. Tax Rate and Capital Stock (Comparative Statics).

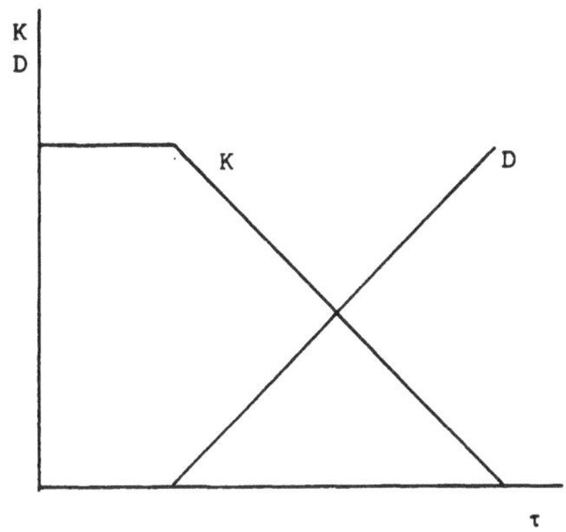

Figure 2. Tax Cut and Fatal Crowding Out.

$iD = 9.26$. Public debt this period plus public consumption and public interest minus tax proceeds yield public debt next period:

(16) $$D_{+1} = D + G + iD - t(Y + iD) = 19.43$$

The portfolio is made up of public debt and private capital $K_{+1} = S - D_{+1} = -7.61$. As a consequence, the stock of capital becomes negative, which economically makes no sense. This outcome can be attributed to two factors, to the reduction in private assets and to the increase in public debt. Put another way, in period 3, the economy will break down.

Table 3 provides an overview of the time path. Initially, in period 0, the economy is in full equilibrium. Then, in period 1, the government cuts down the tax rate. This gives rise to a vicious circle where the government borrows in order to finance the interest payments on public debt. Eventually, in period 3, the economy collapses because of fatal crowding out. What is more, figure 2 displays the process of adjustment (with time τ).

At this stage, the question arises whether the government can cure this process. To answer this question, three possible solutions will be examined here. First: The government lifts the tax rate back to its original value. Second: The government stabilizes public debt at its current level. And third: The government pays off public debt completely.

Table 3
Tax Cut and Fatal Crowding Out

τ	0	1	2	3
t	0.2	0.1	0.1	0.1
K	11.8	11.8	8.0	0
N	100	100	100	100
Y	52.7	52.7	46.9	0
G	10.5	10.5	10.5	0
D	0	0	5.3	
i	1.3	1.3	1.8	
iD	0	0	9.3	
T	10.5	5.3	5.6	
B	0	5.3	14.2	

To begin with, we consider the case that the government restores the tax rate to its original value. Table 4 allows to trace the time path of the model. At the outset, in period 0, the economy is in the steady state. Firms employ 11.8 machines and 100 workers to fabricate 52.7 units. No public debt does exist, and the budget is balanced. Against this background, in period 1, the government lowers the tax rate from 0.2 to 0.1. For the time being, this step leaves no impact on capital, output and public debt. On account of the tax cut, the government runs a budget deficit of 5.3. Up to now, table 4 is identical to table 3.

In order to stop the vicious circle, in period 2, the government raises the tax rate back to 0.2. The stock of capital and thus output have been decided on in the past $K=8.01$ and $Y=46.89$. Both the fall in income and the tax rise contribute to a decline in private savings $S=\beta\delta(1-t)Y=10.50$. Multiply public debt

$D=5.26$ by the rate of interest $i=1.76$ to reach public interest $iD=9.26$. In the subsequent period, public debt builds up to:

(17) $$D_{+1}=D+G+iD-t(Y+iD)=13.82$$

in spite of the tax increase. The reason is that public interest climbs even more. In the portfolio, public debt displaces private capital $K_{+1}=S-D_{+1}=-3.32$. That means, the stock of capital becomes negative, which seems not to be feasible. Finally, in period 3, all economic activities come to a halt. As a result, the fatal process cannot be cured by returning to the initial tax rate.

Next we regard the case that the government stabilizes public debt at its current level. Table 5 displays the corresponding process of adjustment. At the start, in period 0, the economy is in the full equilibrium. Under these circumstances, in period 1, the government reduces the tax rate from 0.2 to 0.1. In full analogy to table 3, public debt tends to explode.

Table 4
Return to Initial Tax Rate

τ	0	1	2	3
t	0.2	0.1	0.2	0.2
K	11.8	11.8	8.0	0
N	100	100	100	100
Y	52.7	52.7	46.9	0
G	10.5	10.5	10.5	0
D	0	0	5.3	
i	1.3	1.3	1.6	
iD	0	0	9.3	
T	10.5	5.3	11.2	
B	0	5.3	8.6	

In order to avoid this, in period 2, the government increases the tax rate so as to balance the budget. From the budget constraint $t(Y+iD)=G+iD$, one can infer the required tax rate:

(18) $$t=\frac{G+iD}{Y+iD}$$

The government pays the interest rate $i=1.76$ on public debt $D=5.26$, so public interest amounts to $iD=9.26$. According to (18), the necessary tax rate equals $t=0.352$. In other words, to keep public debt constant, the government must

Table 5
Stabilization of Public Debt

τ	0	1	2	3	4
t	0.2	0.1	0.35	0.53	
K	11.8	11.8	8.0	3.3	0
N	100	100	100	100	100
Y	52.7	52.7	46.9	35.8	0
G	10.5	10.5	10.5	10.5	0
D	0	0	5.3	5.3	
i	1.3	1.3	1.8	3.3	
iD	0	0	9.3	17.4	
T	10.5	5.3	19.8	27.9	
B	0	5.3	0	0	

raise the tax rate substantially from 0.1 to 0.35. The tax increase and the fall in income combine to lower private savings $S=\beta\delta(1-t)Y=8.51$. A certain proportion of private assets is diverted by public debt, the remainder being left for private capital $K_{+1}=S-D_{+1}=3.25$. Of course, public debt is held fast at the current level of 5.26. Nevertheless, private capital continues to decline, due to the drop in private savings.

At this point, we close period 2 and open up period 3. The decumulation of capital forces firms to contract output $Y=35.77$. The rate of interest goes up to $i=3.30$, as capital becomes scarce. This pushes up public interest to $iD=17.36$, even though public debt does not move. From (18) one can calculate the tax rate which is needed to balance the budget $t=0.525$. The dramatic rise in the tax rate can be ascribed to two factors, to a smaller tax base and to higher public interest. The tax increase along with the reduction in income depresses private savings $S=\beta\delta(1-t)Y=4.76$. Private assets are used to finance public debt and private capital $K_{+1}=S-D_{+1}=-0.5$. Put differently, the stock of capital becomes negative. As a consequence, in period 4, the economy breaks down. To conclude, the government cannot arrest the downward spiral by stabilizing public debt at its current level.

The third strategy consists in retiring public debt altogether. Table 6 explains how the economy evolves over time. At the beginning, in period 0, the economy is in the steady state. Then, in period 1, the government reduces the tax rate from 0.2 to 0.1, thereby throwing the economy out of equilibrium.

In order to bring fatal crowding out to a standstill, in period 2, the government pays off public debt entirely $D_{+1}=0$. More precisely, the government adapts the tax rate so as to cover public debt, public consumption and public interest $t(Y+iD)=D+G+iD$. This provides the necessary tax rate:

(19) $$t=\frac{D+G+iD}{Y+iD}$$

Public debt $D=5.26$ bears the interest rate $i=1.76$, so public interest reaches $iD=9.26$. Hence the government must sharply increase the tax rate from 0.1 to 0.446, thus curbing private savings $S=\beta\delta(1-t)Y=7.27$. Private assets this period give private capital next period $K_{+1}=S=7.27$, public debt being no longer part of the portfolio.

At this stage, we enter period 3. The stock of capital declines, so firms are compelled to restrict output $Y=45.55$. The government accommodates the tax rate such that tax revenue matches public consumption $tY=G$. That is to say, the government may cut down the tax rate to 0.231. As far as private savings are concerned, two opposite forces are at work. On the one hand, the tax cut improves private savings. On the other hand, the drop of income deteriorates private savings. On balance, private savings recover $S=\beta\delta(1-t)Y=9.81$. Private assets determine the stock of capital $K_{+1}=S=9.81$.

Table 6
Repayment of Public Debt

τ	0	1	2	3	4	∞
t	0.2	0.1	0.45	0.23	0.21	0.2
K	11.8	11.8	8.0	7.3	9.8	11.8
N	100	100	100	100	100	100
Y	52.7	52.7	46.9	45.6	49.8	52.7
G	10.5	10.5	10.5	10.5	10.5	10.5
D	0	0	5.3	0	0	0
i	1.3	1.3	1.8	1.9	1.5	1.3
iD	0	0	9.3	0	0	0
T	10.5	5.3	25.1	10.5	10.5	10.5
B	0	5.3	- 5.3	0	0	0

As the stock of capital grows, in period 4, firms can expand output. For that reason, the government is in a position to reduce the tax rate once again $t=0.211$. Correspondingly, private assets and the stock of capital keep on rising $K_{+1}=S=\beta\delta(1-t)Y=11.01$. This virtuous circle continues round by round. As time proceeds ($\tau\to\infty$), the economy approaches the original steady state. Particularly, the tax rate returns to its initial value $t=0.2$. In summary, the redemption of public debt seems to be the only remedy to cure the fatal process.

So far, emphasis has been laid on a reduction in the tax rate. Instead, we shall now address a tax increase. Essentially, the analysis follows the same line as before. Table 7 illuminates the dynamics. At the outset, in period 0, the economy is in the stationary equilibrium. The tax rate has been fixed at $t=0.2$, so there is no public debt. Firms manufacture 52.67 units with the help of 11.80 machines and 100 workers.

In this situation, in period 1, the government lifts the tax rate from 0.2 to 0.3. The stock of capital has been inherited from the past, hence production does not change. However, the tax increase curtails private savings of the young people $S=\beta\delta(1-t)Y=10.32$. In addition, the tax rise moves the budget into surplus, thus public wealth comes into existence $D_{+1}=G-tY=-5.27$. Both private and public assets serve to finance private capital $K_{+1}=S-D_{+1}=15.59$. The government makes loans to the private sector, thereby encouraging private investment.

Then, in period 2, the accumulation of capital allows firms to elevate output $Y=57.26$. On that ground, the initial drop of private savings reverses itself $S=\beta\delta(1-t)Y=11.22$. In mathematical terms, public debt of the current period, augmented by public consumption as well as by public interest and diminished by tax proceeds, establishes public debt of the subsequent period:

$$D_{+1}=D+G+iD-t(Y+iD) \tag{20}$$

The government earns the interest rate $i=1.10$ on public assets $D=-5.27$, so it receives interest payments $iD=-5.80$. That is the main reason why public wealth keeps on rising $D_{+1}=-15.98$. This, together with the increment in private wealth, induces the stock of capital to grow $K_{+1}=S-D_{+1}=27.20$.

Therefore, in period 3, this pushes up output $Y=67.67$ and private savings $S=\beta\delta(1-t)Y=13.26$. Accordingly, public assets $D_{+1}=-34.10$ and private capital $K_{+1}=S-D_{+1}=47.36$ spring up once more. This virtuous circle repeats itself round by round. In the long run, public debt goes to minus infinity. As a consequence, private capital and output tend to explode. Incidentally, the rate of interest converges to zero. Last but not least, figure 3 visualizes the resulting time path of public debt and private capital.

Table 7

Tax Increase and Process of Adjustment

τ	0	1	2	3	∞
t	0.2	0.3	0.3	0.3	0.3
K	11.8	11.8	15.6	27.2	∞
N	100	100	100	100	100
Y	52.7	52.7	57.3	67.7	∞
G	10.5	10.5	10.5	10.5	10.5
D	0	0	- 5.3	- 16.0	- ∞
i	1.3	1.3	1.1	0.7	0
iD	0	0	- 5.8	- 11.9	
T	10.5	15.8	15.4	16.7	
B	0	- 5.3	- 10.7	- 18.1	

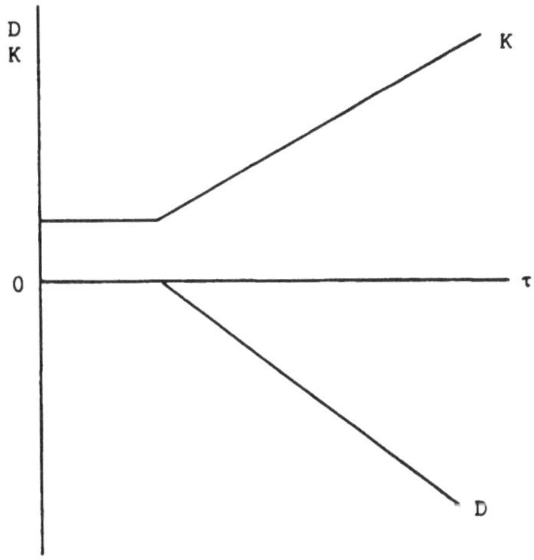

Figure 3. Tax Increase and Process of Adjustment.

3.4 Public Consumption in Utility Function

In the preceding sections, it was implicitly assumed that public consumption does not enter the utility function. In the current section, we shall relax this assumption. It will be demonstrated here that private savings per head are independent of the volume of public consumption. Therefore, the long-run equilibrium proves to be identical.

Apart from this, we take the same approach as before. Regard a stationary economy with public debt. The government buys a specified amount of goods and services $G = \text{const}$. In addition, the government imposes a proportional tax on both factor income and public interest. To simplify matters, let the utility function of the representative household be additive-logarithmic:

(1) $$u = \gamma \log c^1 + \delta \log c^2 + \varepsilon \log G$$

with $\gamma > 0$, $\delta > 0$, $\varepsilon > 0$ and $\gamma + \delta = 1$. Furthermore, households do not rival in the use of public consumption. In full analogy, we obtain the individual budget constraint:

(2) $$c^1 + \frac{c^2}{1 + (1-t)i} = (1-t)w$$

Households select present and future consumption so as to maximize utility subject to their budget constraint $\partial u / \partial c^1 = \partial u / \partial c^2$ or:

(3) $$c^1 = \gamma(1-t)w$$

(4) $$s = \delta(1-t)w$$

Hence public consumption does not affect private savings of the young generation.

Again, private savings per head times the number of active workers give private assets $S = sN$. Then observe $s = \delta(1-t)w$ and $wN = \beta Y$ to arrive at $S = \beta\delta(1-t)Y$. Finally put this into $S = D + K$:

$$D + K = \beta\delta(1-t)Y \tag{5}$$

As a result, public consumption has no influence on public debt and private capital.

To conclude, the long-run equilibrium can be characterized by a system of four equations, which is identical to the system derived above, see (20) until (23) in section 3.1. A necessary condition for this outcome is an additive-logarithmic utility function that exhibits a unit elasticity of substitution. On the other hand, we need not to postulate non-rivalness or $\gamma + \delta = 1$.

4. Process of Adjustment

In the short run, a fiscal expansion increases output. In the long run, however, output shrinks back to zero. Accordingly, in the current chapter, the process of adjustment linking the short period and the long period will be sketched out briefly. Initially, the economy is in the long-run equilibrium. Against this background, suddenly, an investment shock occurs. In order to maintain full employment, the government runs a loose fiscal policy. As a response, the economy passes through the short-run and medium-run equilibrium, ultimately settling down in the long-run equilibrium.

To begin with, in section 4.1., the short-run equilibrium will be complemented by the supply side. Then, in section 4.2., we shall introduce the medium-run equilibrium. There, the accent will be on the demand-side effects of public interest. In section 4.3., we shall extend the long-run equilibrium to include a monetary compartment. Further, in section 4.4., the process of adjustment will be discussed in greater detail. Finally, in section 4.5., we shall look at this process from the perspective of the AD-AS diagram.

4.1. Short-Run Equilibrium

In the current section, aggregate supply will be incorporated into the model. In the short run, money wages are downward rigid. The stock of capital and public debt are given exogenously. Technology is characterized by fixed coefficients, since substitution is a slow process.

Let us begin with aggregate demand. The investigation will be conducted within the familiar IS-LM framework, compare chapter 2 above. Both the goods market and the money market are in equilibrium. Aggregate supply corresponds to aggregate demand, and real balances coincide with the real demand for money:

$$Y = C[(1-t)Y] + I(i) + G \tag{1}$$

$$M/P = L(i, Y) \tag{2}$$

Without loss of generality, we assume that at the start there is no public debt, so the government makes no interest payments.

We come now to aggregate supply. Some methods of production need more labour, while others require more capital. Before setting up a plant, firms can choose among different processes. The decision crucially depends on the ratio between wages and interest. When wages are rather high, firms will use much capital. Conversely, when wages are low, firms will employ many workers. After setting up the plant, however, the capital-labour ratio is fixed. The capital intensity before and after setting up the plant is so to speak like putty and clay.

The revision of the capital-labour ratio must wait until replacement. Suppose the plant has a life of ten years, then the capital intensity can only be corrected after ten years. In the aggregate that means: The capital-labour ratio responds sluggishly to changes in the factor-price ratio. In other words, substitution is a slow process. In the short period, the elasticity of substitution (σ) is small, yet in the long period it is large. This matter of fact will be stylized in the following way: In the short run, technology is characterized by fixed coefficients ($\sigma = 0$), but in the long run the production function is smooth (e.g. $\sigma = 1$).

So far, we considered a shock in the factor-price ratio. Next we shall take a look at how firms answer to a reduction in aggregate demand. In this case, too, the revision of the capital-labour ratio has to wait until replacement. In the short term, inputs cannot be substituted for one another. The stock of capital is constant, so firms put some machines out of operation. What is more, firms lay off some workers. Wage cost can be lowered, but interest cost cannot. That is to say, marginal cost equals unit labour cost. In the long term, however, capital may be substituted for labour, capacity is fully utilized, and unemployment perhaps increases. It turns out once again: Substitution is a slow process.

Firms produce a homogeneous commodity Y by means of capital K and labour N. In the short run, technology exhibits fixed coefficients:

$$Y = \min\left(\frac{K}{v}, \frac{\bar{N}}{a}\right) \tag{3}$$

The capital-output ratio v indicates how many units of capital are necessary to manufacture one unit of output. Analogously, the labour-output ratio a states how much labour is required to produce one unit of output. The input-output ratios are invariant: $v = \text{const}$ and $a = \text{const}$.

In the short period, the stock of capital is given exogenously $K = \text{const}$. Labour supply is also fixed $\bar{N} = \text{const}$, particularly it is not influenced by real wages.

Essentially, the price equation of econometrics suggests two stylized facts, cf. for instance Okun (1981), p. 163, p. 165f. First, variations in aggregate demand in the short run leave no impact on prices. And second, an increase in money wages in the short run leads to a proportionate increase in prices. By which method of pricing can these stylized facts be best explained? Marginal-cost pricing proves to be ruinous under fixed coefficients. Average-cost pricing clearly contradicts the stylized facts: When aggregate demand rises, prices will fall. And the other way round, when aggregate demand declines, prices will go up.

A third approach consists of normal-cost pricing. Firms set the price equal to normal unit cost, which is the short-run expectation of unit costs:

$$P = aw\,(1 + z) \qquad (4)$$

Here w stands for the money wage rate, aw denotes unit labour cost, and z – const ist the markup rate. Firms mark up unit labour cost to allow for fixed cost. When the current level of aggregate demand deviates from its expected value, firms will not alter the price. On the other hand, in the case of a wage rise, there will be a proportionate price adjustment. Obviously, normal-cost pricing agrees with the stylized facts, so it will be postulated henceforth. The microfoundation of normal-cost pricing heavily draws on the theory of monopolistic competition, see Weitzman (1985).

In the preceding analysis, we supposed that aggregate demand governs output. Now we shall take account of the fact that production is restricted by the stock of capital and by labour supply. Capacity output is by definition that volume of production, at which the stock of capital is fully utilized:

$$\bar{Y}_K = \frac{K}{v} \qquad (5)$$

Full-employment output, analogously, is that volume of production, at which all workers find a job:

$$\bar{Y}_N = \frac{\bar{N}}{a} \qquad (6)$$

Therefore, actual output Y is the minimum of aggregate demand Y_o, capacity output and full-employment output:

$$Y = \min\,(Y_o, \bar{Y}_K, \bar{Y}_N) \qquad (7)$$

Accordingly, either a lack of aggregate demand, a capital shortage or a scarcity of workers may happen. Firms engage as many workers as they need to produce output. Strictly speaking, under fixed coefficients, labour demand N is proportional to output:

$$N = aY \qquad (8)$$

Figure 1 shows the full-employment line and the capacity line in the IS-LM diagram. In the case depicted there, neither restriction is binding. The economy suffers from unemployment, and part of capacity lies idle.

Having laid this groundwork, we come next to the functioning of the short-run equilibrium. First of all, it is convenient to posit for the moment that

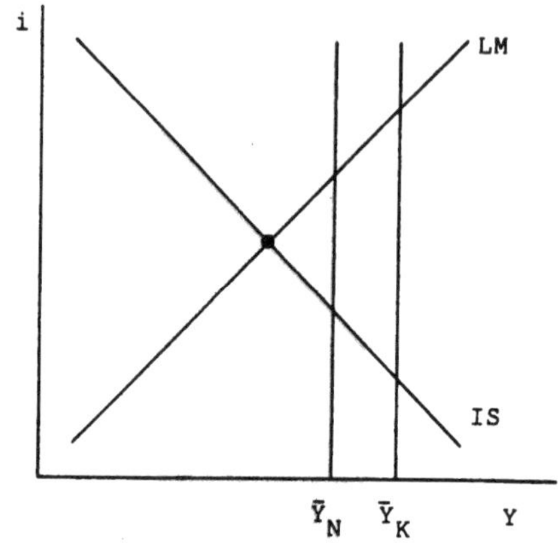

Figure 1. Full-Employment Line and Capacity Line.

capacity harmonizes with full employment $\bar{Y} = \bar{Y}_K = \bar{Y}_N$. Now the short-run equilibrium can be represented by a system of four equations:

(9) $$Y = C\,[(1-t)Y] + I(i) + G$$

(10) $$M/P = L(i, Y)$$

(11) $$P = aw\,(1+z)$$

(12) $$N = aY$$

In the short run, money wages are downward rigid. This gives rise to two cases, depending on the state of the labour market. When labour demand falls short of labour supply $N < \bar{N}$, money wages will not decline. Conversely, when labour demand exceeds labour supply $N > \bar{N}$, money wages will increase so as to clear the labour market $N = \bar{N}$.

Let us begin with a situation of unemployment $N < \bar{N}$. In this case, a, t, w, z, G, and M are given exogenously, while i, N, P and Y are endogenous variables. There are as many equations as unknowns, so the system from (9) until (12) is definite. What is more, the system can be solved recursively. Take equation (11) as a starting point, from which P immediately emerges. Then insert this into (9) and (10) to obtain i and Y. Finally eliminate Y in (12).

We turn now to a situation of full employment $N = \bar{N}$. In this case, money wages become endogenous, whereas labour demand becomes exogenous. Above all, equation (12) determines Y. This together with (9) provides i. Then substitute Y and i into (10) to arrive at P. Eventually one can deduce w from (11).

Properly speaking, most of the variables mentioned above are defined in real terms. For example, Y symbolizes real output (real income), C is real consumption, and I is real investment. The only exceptions to this rule are given by the money wage rate w and by the nominal quantity of money M.

Figure 2 illustrates the short-run effects of a reduction in aggregate demand. Suppose that at the outset there is full employment. The initial equilibrium is characterized by the common point of intersection of the *IS* curve, the *LM* curve and the $\bar{Y}$ vertical. Now imagine that aggregate demand declines autonomously. This disturbance shifts the *IS* curve to the left, while the other curves stay in their original position. As a consequence, unemployment comes into existence.

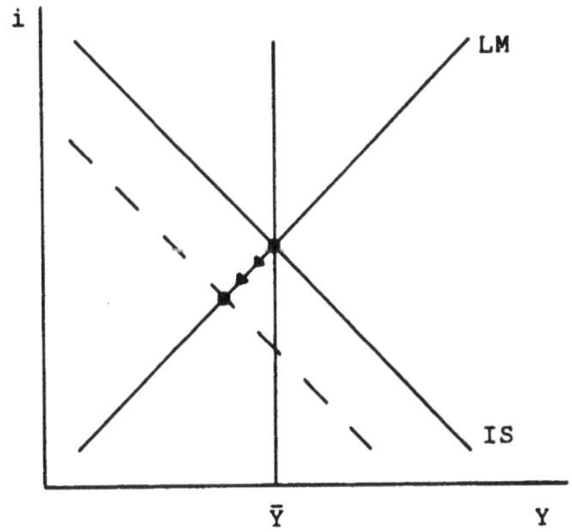

Figure 2. Reduction in Aggregate Demand.

Figure 3, by way of contrast, displays the short-period impact of an increase in aggregate demand. At the start, again, all workers have got a job. Once more, the initial equilibrium lies in the intersection of the goods-market schedule, of the money-market schedule and of the full-employment line. Under these circumstances, aggregate demand expands spontaneously. This shock moves the *IS*-curve to the right, thereby causing overemployment. As a quick response,

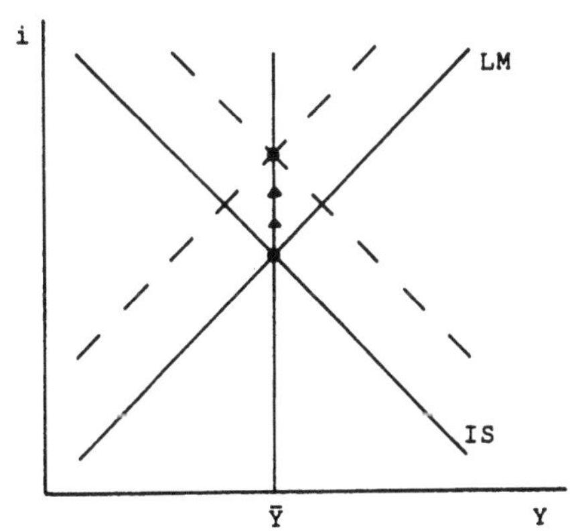

Figure 3. Increase in Aggregate Demand.

money wages spring up. On account of the rise in normal unit cost, firms mark up prices. This measure lowers real balances, thus driving up the rate of interest. For that reason, private investment diminishes, so ultimately firms contract output. This is the familiar Keynes effect. In the diagram, the *LM* curve goes to the left. This process continues until full employment is restored up the $\bar{Y}$ vertical.

4.2. Medium-Run Equilibrium

In the current section, the demand-side effects of public interest will be included into the analysis. At the beginning, let the government run a budget deficit, so public debt builds up. Accordingly, the government must pay more interest round by round, which enhances disposable income, private consumption and thus aggregate demand.

The medium-run equilibrium can be condensed to a system of four equations, as far as the demand side is concerned:

$$Y = C[(1-t)(Y+iD)] + I(i) + G \tag{1}$$

$$M/P = L(i, Y) \tag{2}$$

$$B = G + iD - t(Y+iD) \tag{3}$$

$$D_{+1} = D + B \tag{4}$$

On the one hand, the government borrows in order to finance the interest payments on public debt. On the other hand, the government levies a proportional tax on public interest.

4.3. Long-Run Equilibrium

In the long run, money wages are downward flexible. The stock of capital and public debt accommodate themselves appropriately. The production function indeed is smooth. Principally, we shall take the same approach as before. The long-run equilibrium will again be based on an overlapping generations model without bequest. The only difference here is, that the real analysis of chapter 3 will be supplemented by a monetary analysis.

Firms seek to maximize profits Π under perfect competition:

$$\Pi = PY - iPK - wN \tag{1}$$

where w denotes the money rate of wages. Differentiate (1) for K, set the derivative equal to zero and regroup:

$$i = \frac{\partial Y}{\partial K} = \frac{\alpha Y}{K} \tag{2}$$

That means, the interest rate corresponds to the marginal product of capital. Besides differentiate (1) for N to obtain:

(3) $$\frac{w}{P}=\frac{\partial Y}{\partial N}=\frac{\beta Y}{N}$$

Put another way, the real rate of wages agrees with the marginal product of labour.

The next point refers to the money market. The central bank controls the nominal supply of money $M=\text{const}$. In addition, the real demand for money is a declining function of the interest rate and an increasing function of income: $L=L(i, Y)$ with $L_1<0$ and $L_2>0$. The money market is in equilibrium, hence real balances match the real demand for money:

(4) $$\frac{M}{P}=L(i, Y)$$

In summary, the long-run equilibrium can be described by a system of six equations:

(5) $$Y=K^{\alpha}N^{\beta}$$
(6) $$i=\alpha Y/K$$
(7) $$w/P=\beta Y/N$$
(8) $$D+K=\beta\delta(1-t)Y$$
(9) $$G+iD=t\,(Y+iD)$$
(10) $$M/P=L(i, Y)$$

Here α, β, δ, t, G, M and N are given exogenously, while i, w, D, K, P and Y are endogenous variables. There are as many equations as unknowns, so the system can be solved. Further, equations (5), (6), (8) and (9) are identical to equations (20) until (23) in section 3.1. Therefore, the two models coincide in real terms. In other words, money seems to be neutral in this context. As a result, a long-run equilibrium does indeed exist. Unfortunately, however, it proves to be unstable, as has already been established in section 3.2.

4.4. Process of Adjustment

In the current section, the process of adjustment will be examined more closely. The analysis will be carried out with the help of the *IS-LM* diagram. Initially, the economy is in the long-run equilibrium. Then, suddenly, an investment shock occurs. In order to maintain full employment, the government runs a loose fiscal policy. As a response, the economy passes through the short-run and medium-run equilibrium, finally settling down in the new long-run equilibrium.

Figures 1 and 2 illustrate the short-term and medium-term effects of fiscal policy. At the beginning, the economy is in the steady state. The common point of intersection of the IS curve, the LM curve and the $\bar{Y}$ vertical marks the long-run equilibrium, see figure 1. Capacity harmonizes with full employment $\bar{Y} = \bar{Y}_K = \bar{Y}_N$. All workers have got a job $Y = \bar{Y}$. Firms do not invest $I = 0$, so the stock of capital does not change. The budget is balanced $B = 0$. At the start, let there be no public debt $D = 0$, without losing generality. Accordingly, public consumption agrees with tax revenue $G = tY$.

Under these circumstances, abruptly, an investment shock occurs. Sales expectations worsen, thus firms reduce autonomous investment. In figure 1, the IS curve shifts to the left. This gives rise to unemployment and brings the budget into deficit. Besides, net investment becomes negative. In order to reestablish full employment, the government pursues a fiscal expansion. It increases public consumption, thereby moving the IS curve to the right. Strictly speaking, the IS curve comes back into its original position. On the other hand, this action reinforces the budget deficit. The rate of interest goes up, which further depresses private investment.

In the short-period equilibrium, again, all workers find a job. What is more, net investment is negative, and the government runs a budget deficit.

At this point, we leave the short-run impact of fiscal policy and turn to the medium-run consequences, see figure 2. Owing to the budget deficit, public debt builds up round by round. The accompanying increase in public interest enhances disposable income, private consumption and aggregate demand. For that reason, the IS schedule shifts to the right. Since there was full employment, money wages will climb so as to clear the labour market. This compels firms to

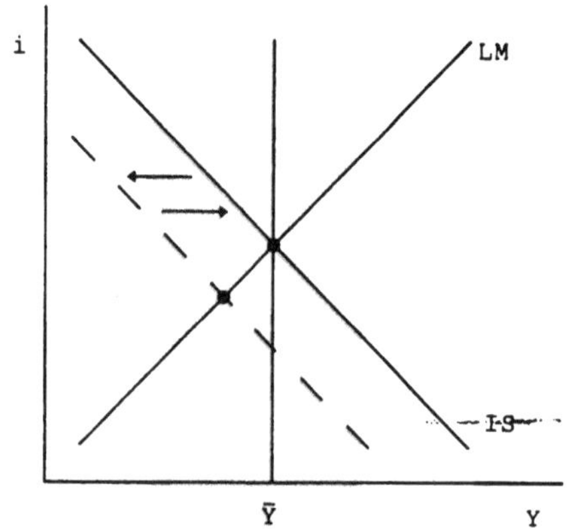

Figure 1. Short-Run Effects of Fiscal Policy.

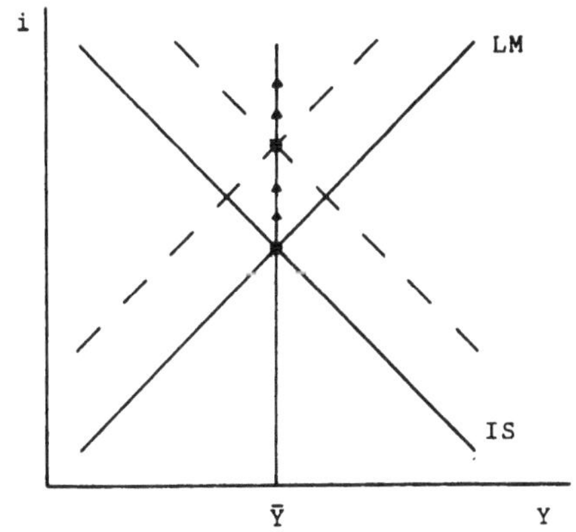

Figure 2. Medium-Run Effects of Fiscal Policy.

raise prices, thereby lowering real balances. On that account, the *LM* schedule moves to the left.

In addition, the rise in the interest rate and the rise in public debt combine to a further rise in public interest. In order to finance this, the government has to borrow even more. The ensuing increase in the budget deficit speeds up the accumulation of public debt. Period by period, the *IS* curve goes to the right, while the *LM* curve goes to the left.

Moreover, the dramatic rise in the rate of interest displaces private investment. That is to say, net investment becomes even more negative. Due to this, the stock of capital declines round by round. Correspondingly, capacity output falls, thus limiting actual output. In figure 2, the full-employment line travels to the left. Besides, the reduction in income causes a reduction in tax proceeds. On that ground, the government must raise even more loans, hence the growth of public debt accelerates once again.

In the long run, as a result, public debt tends to explode, which drives private capital down to zero. Eventually, there will be fatal crowding out.

Figure 3 graphs how output evolves over time. Initially, the investment shock contracts output. In the short run, the fiscal expansion replenishes output. In the long run, however, it squeezes output to zero. Ultimately, therefore, the economy will break down.

Here the question arises, whether the government can stop this vicious circle. As potential answers, we shall try out the medium-run adjustment of fiscal and monetary policy, respectively.

At first, have a look at fiscal policy, compare figure 4. More exactly, let us return to the medium-run influence of fiscal policy. As a starting point, take the fact that the budget deficit augments public debt. The subsequent rise in public

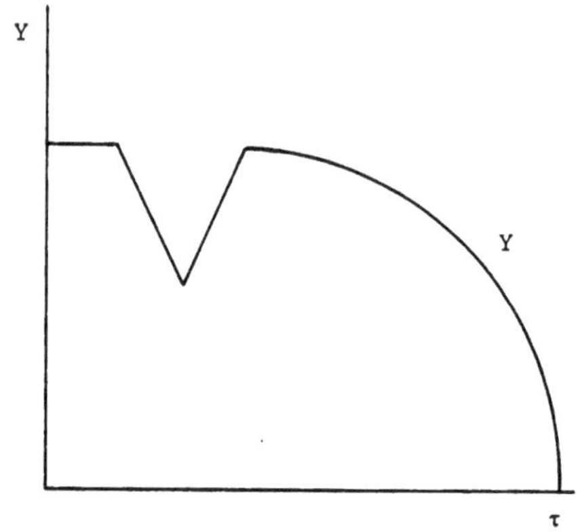

Figure 3. Time Path of Output and Ultimate Breakdown.

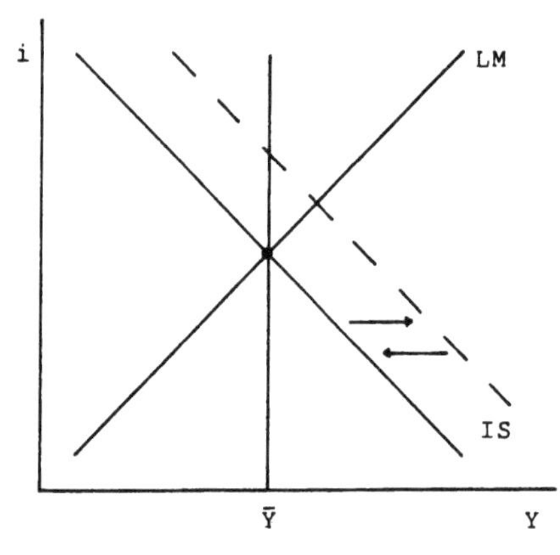

Figure 4. Medium-Run Adjustment of Fiscal Policy.

interest steps up disposable income and private consumption. This effect pushes the *IS* schedule to the right. In order to prevent overemployment from coming into existence, the government adapts fiscal policy. In other words, it cuts down public consumption, thus pulling the *IS* schedule back to the left.

What are the long-run consequences of this strategy? This problem will now be explored in greater detail. The goods market is known to be in equilibrium:

(1) $$Y = C[(1-t)(Y+R)] + I(i) + G$$

R is shorthand for public interest $R = iD$. During the medium-run adjustment of fiscal policy, the government wishes to keep up full employment $\Delta Y = 0$.

Accordingly, (1) can be expressed in terms of differences as $0 = c(1-t)\Delta R + \Delta G$, where c stands for the marginal propensity to consume. Then solve this equation for:

(2) $$\Delta G = -c(1-t)\Delta R$$

That means, an increase in public interest leads to a reduction in public consumption.

Further regard the budget constraint:

(3) $$B = G + R - t(Y+R)$$

In full analogy, take differences of (3):

(4) $$\Delta B = \Delta G + (1-t)\Delta R$$

Finally insert (2) into (4) to obtain:

(5) $$\Delta B = (1-c)(1-t)\Delta R$$

From this one can deduce that a rise in public interest implies a rise in public borrowing.

In summary, we arrive at a fatal process. The given budget deficit builds up public debt period by period, which goes along with a swell in public interest. To compensate for this expansionary effect, the government must lower public consumption. In spite of this, the budget deficit becomes larger. Hence the growth of public debt and public interest speeds up. To curb aggregate demand, the government must contract public consumption once again. This process repeats itself round by round. At a particular point in time, public consumption vanishes altogether $G = 0$. Thereafter it turns negative, which economically makes no sense. As a result, the medium-run adjustment of fiscal policy cannot be sustained. Put another way, the government is not able to halt the downward spiral.

Last but not least, we shall address the medium-run adjustment of monetary policy, confer figure 5. The demand-side effect of public interest is inflationary, as has been demonstrated above. In order to fight this "fiscal inflation", should the central bank switch over to a monetary contraction?

In the intermediate period, the accumulation of public debt raises public interest, thus supporting disposable income and private consumption. In figure 5, the *IS* curve shifts to the right. To check the resulting demand-pull inflation, the central bank runs a policy of tight money. Accordingly, the *LM* curve moves to the left. On the one hand, this measure stabilizes prices at the current level. On the other hand, it amplifies the increase in the rate of interest. Private investment falls even more, so the decline of capital accelerates. To conclude, the medium-run accommodation of monetary policy seems not to be reasonable.

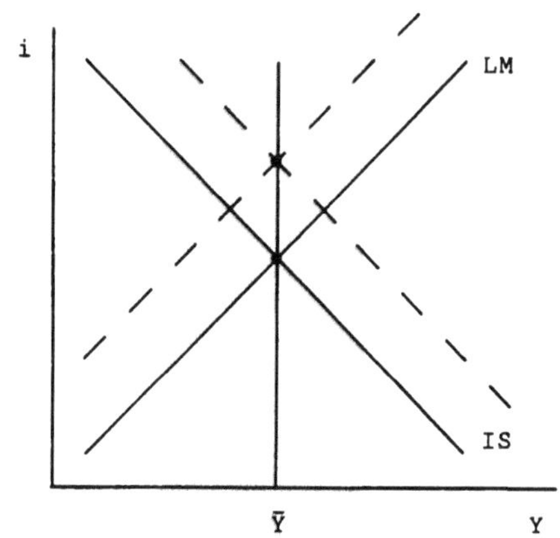

Figure 5. Medium-Run Adjustment of Monetary Policy.

4.5. AD-AS Diagram

Throughout the monograph, as a rule, we rely on the IS-LM diagram. In the present section, instead, the trajectory will be visualized by means of the AD-AS diagram. The aggregate demand curve (AD curve) ist based on the familiar IS-LM analysis. The aggregate supply curve (AS curve) rests on the assumption of fixed coefficients. Then, the point of intersection between the AD curve and the AS curve marks the short-run equilibrium.

First of all the AD curve will be introduced. A price increase causes a reduction of real balances, so the interest rate goes up. As a consequence, private investment and aggregate demand come down. This is the well-known Keynes effect. Accordingly, figure 1 shows the downward sloping AD curve. What is more, the horizontal AS curve plots the price equation $P = aw(1+z)$.

The point of intersection between the AD curve and the AS curve characterizes the short-run equilibrium Y_0, see figure 1. Firms set the price equal to normal unit cost and produce the quantity asked for at this price. They engage as many workers as they need to cover aggregate demand. In addition, figure 1 displays the vertical full-employment line (capacity line). In the case depicted there, the supply-side constraint is not operative.

Now what is the short-term impact of variations in aggregate demand? Let us begin with a decline in aggregate demand, compare figure 2. Initially there is full employment. Against this background, aggregate demand falls autonomously. For that reason, the AD curve shifts to the left. Firms have to lay off workers.

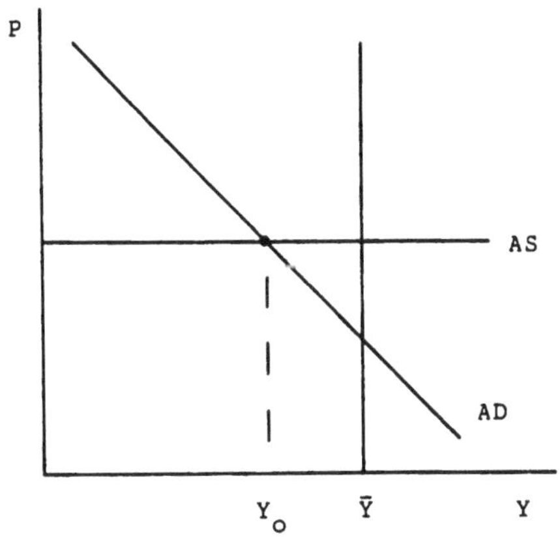

Figure 1. Short-Run Equilibrium.

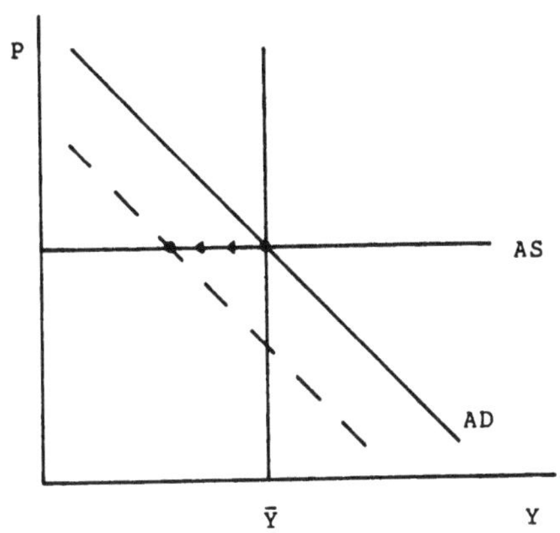

Figure 2. Reduction in Aggregate Demand.

Next consider an increment in aggregate demand, confer figure 3. At the start, again, all workers have got a job. In this situation, aggregate demand rises spontaneously. On that account, the AD curve moves to the right. Overemployment emerges, hence money wages spring up. This forces firms to raise prices, thereby lowering real balances. The interest rate climbs, which depresses private investment and output. Correspondingly, the AS curve glides upwards. In the short-period equilibrium, all workers find a job; only prices have changed.

In the next step, the process of adjustment will be sketched out briefly. At the outset, the economy is in the steady state. The common point of intersection of the AD schedule, of the AS schedule and of the $\bar{Y}$ vertical indicates the initial equilibrium, see figure 4. The labour market clears, and firms abstain from investment $I=0$. The government budget is balanced $B=0$. For the moment, let there be no public debt $D=0$, so the budget constraint simplifies to $G=tY$.

Then, suddenly, an investment shock disrupts the steady state. Sales expectations deteriorate, hence firms cut down autonomous investment. This disturbance pushes the AD curve to the left. The economy suffers from unemployment, and the budget gets into deficit. In order to bring back full employment, the government elevates public consumption. Due to this, the AD curve is pulled back into its original position. As a byproduct, this action widens the budget deficit. In the short-run equilibrium, all workers find a job. The government runs a budget deficit, and firms do disinvest.

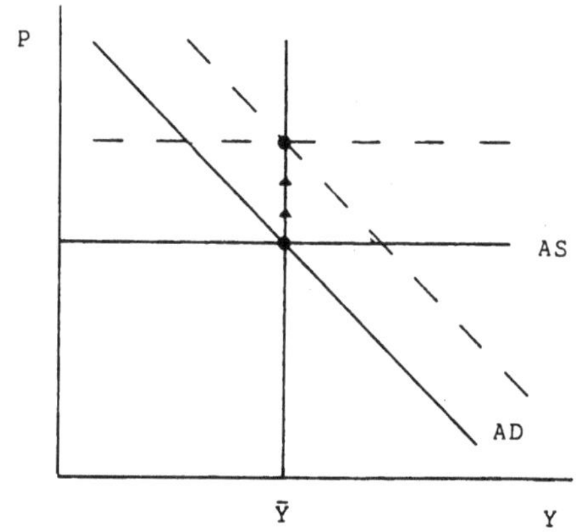

Figure 3. Increase in Aggregate Demand.

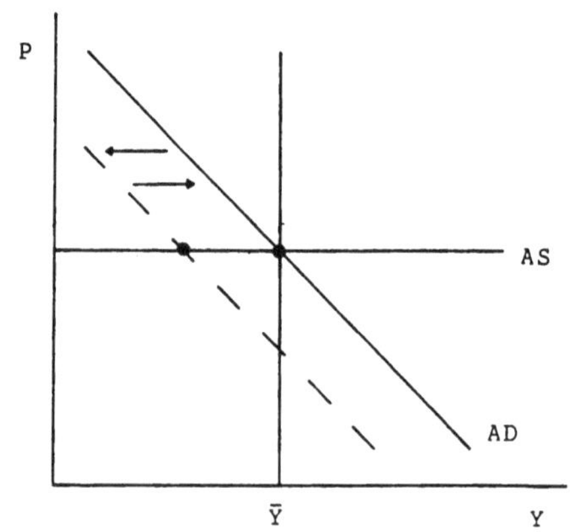

Figure 4. Short-Run Effects of Fiscal Policy.

In the intermediate run, the budget deficit augments public debt. The accompanying upsurge in public interest stimulates private consumption and aggregate demand. Owing to that, the AD curve shifts further to the right, see figure 5. As a consequence, overemployment comes into existence. Money wages and prices go up, thereby curtailing real balances. Accordingly, the AS curve moves upwards. Besides, the rise in the interest rate multiplies the rise in public interest. The government must borrow to finance the interest payments on public debt. This process reiterates itself round by round.

Over and above this, the increase in the rate of interest impairs private investment once angain. In other words, net investment becomes even more negative. The subsequent decline in the stock of capital and in capacity output restricts actual output. In the diagram, the $\bar{Y}$ vertical travels to the left. In the long run, the stock of capital and output converge to zero. Ultimately, the economy will collapse.

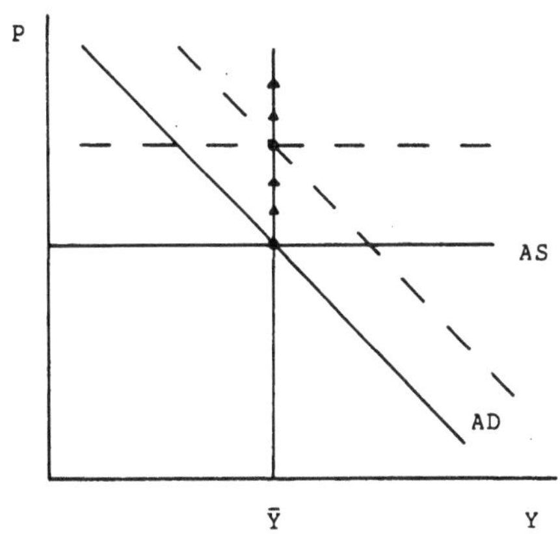

Figure 5. Medium-Run Effects of Fiscal Policy.

5. Investment Shock and Cyclical Adjustment

In the short run, a loose fiscal policy improves output. But in the long run, it brings output down to zero. Judging from this, the long-term cost of fiscal policy seems to be forbidding. On the other hand, this raises the question whether the analysis done so far is really appropriate. Therefore, in chapters 5 and 6, it will be argued that an investment shock induces a cyclical process of adjustment. This in turn calls for a cyclical path of fiscal policy. As a fundamental result, the budget will be balanced over the cycle.

The current chapter is organized as follows. To begin with, in section 5.1., we shall regard an economy without public sector. Then, in section 5.2., the government will enter the model. Properly speaking, the government runs a passive fiscal policy. Instead, in section 5.3., we shall postulate that the government pursues an active fiscal policy. Finally, in section 5.4., alternative paths of adjustment will be evaluated.

5.1. Economy Without Public Sector

The underlying idea can be explained with the help of figure 1. Initially, the economy is in the steady state. All workers have got a job, and firms abstain from investment. Under these circumstances, an investment shock happens. Sales expectations worsen, so the IS curve shifts to the left. In the short-run equilibrium, private investment is negative, hence the stock of capital declines.

The steady state after disturbance is identical to the steady state before disturbance, because all parameters of the stationary equilibrium are constant. Thus, in the long run, the IS curve must come back to its original position. Again, all workers find a job. Firms do not invest, and the terminal stock of capital coincides with the initial stock of capital.

During the process of adjustment, however, firms did disinvest. As a logical consequence, the terminal stock of capital should fall short of the initial stock of capital. In other words, the process of adjustment as set out above must of necessity be incomplete. There must be a phase during which firms do invest to replenish the stock of capital.

This problem will now be looked into more closely. In section 5.1.1., we shall start with the overlapping generations model. There, the focus will be on the long-run equilibrium. Then, in section 5.1.2., we shall introduce the multiplier-accelerator model. In that place, emphasis will be laid on the process of adjustment. At the end, we shall tie up these two approaches.

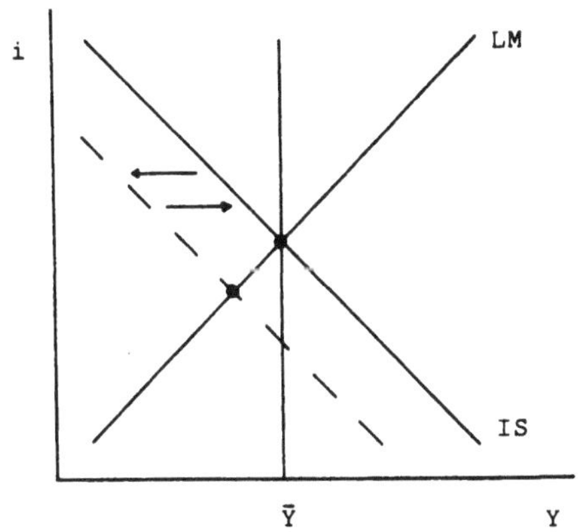

Figure 1. Investment Shock: Short-Run Equilibrium and Long-Run Equilibrium.

5.1.1. Overlapping Generations Model

The long-run equilibrium without public sector can be described by a system of two equations, see (20) until (23) in section 3.1.:

(1) $$Y = K^{\alpha} N^{\beta}$$

(2) $$K = \beta \delta Y$$

Here α, β, δ and N are given exogenously, while K and Y are endogenous variables. There are as many equations as unknowns, so the system is determinate.

As an exception, the long-run equilibrium without government activities can explicitly be solved for the endogenous variables. Substitute (2) into (1) and rearrange:

(3) $$Y = (\beta \delta)^{\alpha / \beta} N$$

Further eliminate Y in (2) by making use of (3):

(4) $$K = (\beta \delta)^{1 / \beta} N$$

As a result, full employment always prevails. Labour supply, the stock of capital and output remain unchanged. Firms do not invest $I = 0$, and households consume the whole of income $C = Y$. This is a stationary economy that tends to a stationary equilibrium where it reproduces itself period by period.

At the beginning, let the economy be in the long-run equilibrium. Now imagine that an investment shock occurs which proves to be transitory. Sales expectations deteriorate autonomously, at least for the moment. As time proceeds, the economy converges to the new long-run equilibrium. Obviously, the steady state after disturbance agrees with the steady state before disturbance, since all parameters are invariant. During the process of adjustment, nothing happens. The reason is that, within this framework, firms have no problem to sell their output. Yet in the short run, this assumption seems to be quite heroic.

5.1.2. Multiplier-Accelerator Model

The current section offers the real analysis of a stationary economy. The investigation will be carried out within an augmented multiplier-accelerator model. We shall start with the short-run equilibrium and after that turn to the long-run equilibrium.

Let us begin with the short-run equilibrium. Output corresponds to private consumption plus private investment $Y = C + I$, so the goods market clears. Private consumption is a linear function of income $C = \bar{C} + cY$ with autonomous consumption $\bar{C} > 0$ and marginal propensity to consume $0 < c < 1$. Private investment serves to fill the gap between the desired stock of capital K^* and the actual stock of capital K step by step: $I = \lambda(K^* - K)$. Here λ symbolizes the speed of adjustment. The desired stock of capital equals expected sales E times the capital-output ratio $K^* = vE$. In the most simple case, expected sales this period are given by actual sales last period $E = Y_{-1}$. Private investment, in turn, adds to the stock of capital $K_{+1} = K + I$.

In summary, the short-run equilibrium can be represented by a system of six equations:

(1) $$Y = C + I$$

(2) $$C = \bar{C} + cY$$

(3) $$I = \lambda(K^* - K)$$

(4) $$K^* = vE$$

(5) $$E = Y_{-1}$$

(6) $$K_{+1} = K + I$$

At this point, we leave the short-run equilibrium and come to the long-run equilibrium. In the long term, the stock of capital does not move $K_{+1} = K$. This together with (6) implies that firms do not invest:

(7) $$I = 0$$

Now insert this together with (2) into (1) and reshuffle:

(8) $$Y = \frac{\bar{C}}{1 - c}$$

That means, the stationary level of income is independent of sales expectations.

Next compare (5) with $Y = Y_{-1}$ to arrive at $E = Y$ or

(9) $$E = \frac{\bar{C}}{1 - c}$$

Within this setting, expected sales play a double role. On the one hand, there may be shocks in sales expectations. On the other hand, in the long period, sales expectations adapt themselves appropriately. Further, (3) and (7) yield $K^* = K$. Substitute this together with $E = Y$ into (4) to get $K = vY$. Finally eliminate Y by means of (8):

$$K = \frac{v\bar{C}}{1-c} \tag{10}$$

Besides, we posit a technology with fixed coefficients:

$$Y = \min\left(\frac{K}{v}, \frac{\bar{N}}{a}\right) \tag{11}$$

If the resource constraint is binding, it will do so only in a soft way. When net investment becomes negative, firms stop the replacement of worn-out facilities. Strictly speaking, the old machines are only put out of operation but not scrapped. Thus they can again be put into use as occasion arises. What is more, firms can operate at maximum capacity instead of at optimum capacity. In the long run, of course, firms will work at optimum capacity. As far as labour is concerned, we may think of overtime and extrashifts.

We suppose that in the long-run equilibrium before disturbance there is full employment. Accordingly, it can be inferred from $Y = \bar{N}/a$ and (8):

$$\bar{C} = \frac{(1-c)\bar{N}}{a} \tag{12}$$

Let this condition be met. Owing to technology (11), firms engage as many workers as they need to cover aggregate demand $N = aY$. During the process of adjustment, therefore, overtime and extrashifts may occur to a certain extent.

Now we assume that initially the economy is in the steady state. In this situation, an investment shock takes place which proves to be temporary. Expected sales come down, at least for the time being. In the long run, as a response, the economy will tend to a new steady state. The long-run equilibrium after disturbance is identical to the long-run equilibrium before disturbance, as has been demonstrated above. Output, the stock of capital and labour demand do not vary over the process of adjustment as a whole. As a result, all workers will find a job. The reason is that all parameters of the model are constant and that sales expectations accommodate themselves.

Last but not least, what is the relationship between the multiplier-accelerator model and the overlapping generations model? We postulate that both models agree in the pre-shock steady state. Then, as a consequence, they agree in the post-shock steady state, too. In this sense, the two models harmonize. What is more, the multiplier-accelerator model specifies the process of adjustment. Put differently, money wages and prices need not to be adapted.

Finally we shall confront the two long-run equilibria. The evaluation of $K = \beta\delta Y$ (overlapping generations model) and $K = vY$ (multiplier-accelerator model) provides:

$$v = \beta\delta \tag{13}$$

In full analogy, the comparison of $Y = (\beta\delta)^{\alpha/\beta}\,\bar{N}$ and $Y = \bar{N}/a$ yields:

$$a = (\beta\delta)^{-\alpha/\beta} \tag{14}$$

5.1.3. Simulation

In the present section, we shall simulate the process of adjustment caused by an investment shock. Accordingly, table 8 provides a synopsis of the resulting time path. The numerical example will be based on the following parameter values: $c = 0.5$, $\bar{C} = 50$, $v = 1$, $\lambda = 0.2$, $a = 1$ and $\bar{N} = 100$. The parameter values have been chosen in such a way that the multiplier amounts to 2. In the long-run equilibrium, output, the stock of capital and labour demand equal 100. The proof goes like this: $Y = \bar{C}/(1-c) = 100$, $K = vY = 100$ and $N = aY = 100$. Hence full employment prevails.

Initially, in period 0, the economy is in the steady state. Firms produce a homogeneous commodity $Y = 100$ by means of capital $K = 100$ and labour $N = 100$. All workers have got a job. Households consume income altogether $C = 100$, and firms do not invest $I = 0$.

Against this background, in period 1, an investment shock occurs. More precisely, expected sales come down autonomously from 100 to 90. For that reason, the desired stock of capital declines from 100 to 90, too. The actual stock of capital has been inherited from the past, so it does not respond immediately. In other words, there is a gap of -10 between the desired stock of capital and the actual stock of capital. According to the speed of adjustment 0.2, private investment falls from 0 to -2. With a multiplier of 2, output drops from 100 to 96. That is to say, the reduction in expected sales leads to a reduction in actual sales. So this is a case of self-fulfilling prophecy. What is more, labour demand is cut back from 100 to 96. As a consequence, unemployment emerges.

At this point, we close period 1 and open up period 2. The experience gained in period 1 induces a rise in expected sales from 90 to 96. On that account, the desired stock of capital also increases from 90 to 96. By way of contrast, the actual stock of capital shrinks from 100 to 98, since net investment was negative in period 1. Thus the accelerator implies that private investment climbs from -2 to -0.4. Therefore, firms expand output from 96 to 99.2. Correspondingly, labour demand goes up from 96 to 99.2.

It is worth noting that output now exceeds the stock of capital. How can this be defended under fixed coefficients? The old machines have only been put out of operation, but not scrapped. So they will again be put into use as occasion

Table 8
Investment Shock and Cyclical Adjustment

τ	E	K*	K	I	Y
0	100	100	100	0	100
1	90	90	100	- 2	96
2	96	96	98	- 0.4	99.2
3	99.2	99.2	97.6	0.3	100.6
4	100.6	100.6	97.9	0.5	101.1
5	101.1	101.1	98.4	0.5	101.1
6	101.1	101.1	98.9	0.4	100.9
7	100.9	100.9	99.3	0.3	100.6
8	100.6	100.6	99.6	0.2	100.4
9	100.4	100.4	99.8	0.1	100.2
10	100.2	100.2	99.9	0.1	100.1
11	100.1	100.1	100	0	100
12	100	100	100	0	100

arises. In addition, firms can operate at maximum capacity instead of at optimum capacity. Besides, there will be overtime and extrashifts.

Here we leave period 2 and enter period 3. To begin with, expected sales improve from 96 to 99.2. Analogously, the desired stock of capital builds up from 96 to 99.2. In spite of this, the actual stock of capital diminishes from 98 to 97.6. For the first time, the desired stock of capital surpasses the actual stock of capital. On that ground, net investment becomes positive. More exactly, private investment increases from -0.4 to $+0.3$. As a response, firms step up production from 99.2 to 100.6. Along the same lines, labour demand rises from 99.2 to 100.6. That means, the economy switches over from underemployment to overemployment.

Properly speaking, labour demand is above labour supply. At first glance, this seems to be incompatible with fixed coefficients. However, with respect to labour, we may think of overtime and extrashifts as well. Further it might be suspected that overemployment is inflationary. We shall assume here that this will not happen. Overemployment is slight and does exist only during a short interval.

This process repeats itself round by round. Finally, in period 12, firms make use of capital $K=100$ and labour $N=100$ to manufacture $Y=100$ units. All workers find a job. Private consumption agrees with income $C=100$, and private investment vanishes $I=0$. Put differently, the economy is again in a steady state. Moreover, the terminal equilibrium coincides with the initial equilibrium.

Figure 1 shows the cyclical path of output. At the start, the economy moves at the full-employment level. Then, suddenly, an investment shock takes place, which drives output down. As time proceeds, output comes up again. At a certain point in time, it rises well above the full-employment value. Eventually, output falls back to the initial level.

Figure 2 illustrates the concomitant path of private investment. At the outset, firms abstain from investment. The disturbance in expectations makes net investment at first negative and later on positive. At the end, firms do not longer invest. This is clearly reflected in the time path of capital, see figure 3. The negative investment lowers the stock of capital, while the positive investment raises the stock of capital back to its initial value.

Essentially, the process of adjustment can be divided into two phases, compare figure 4. At the beginning, the economy is in the long-run equilibrium. The labour market clears. Firms refrain from investment, so the stock of capital is invariant. In the first phase, sales expectations worsen exogenously. For that reason, firms postpone the replacement of capital. In figure 4, accordingly, the IS curve shifts to the left. Net investment becomes negative, hence the stock of capital declines round by round. As a consequence, firms have to dismiss workers, thereby creating unemployment.

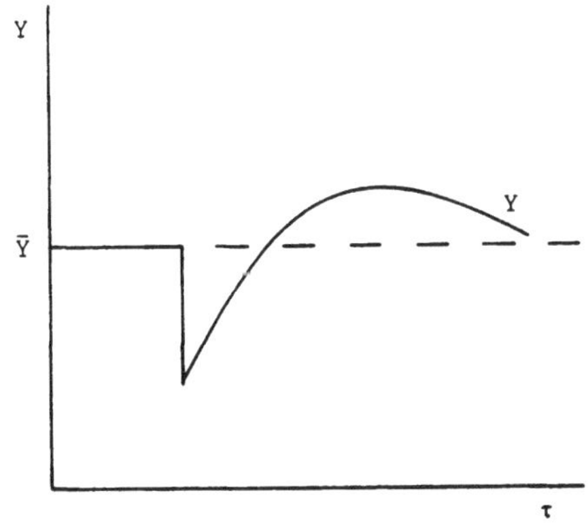

Figure 1. Cyclical Path of Output.

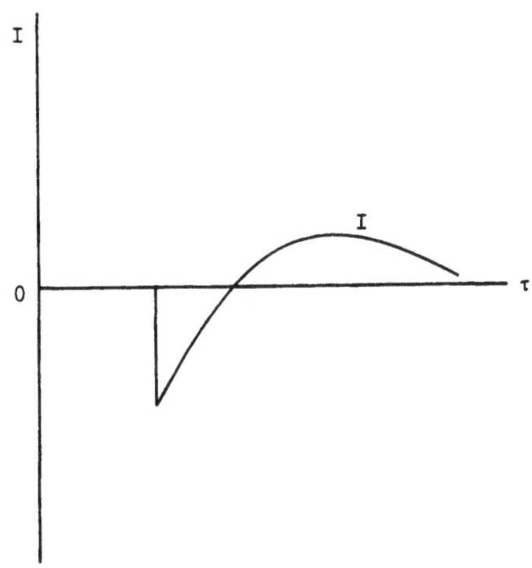

Figure 2. Cyclical Path of Private Investment.

In the second phase, sales expectations recover endogenously. Firms make good the replacement of capital. In figure 4, the IS curve substantially moves to the right. Net investment springs up, thus increasing the stock of capital round by round. Therefore, underemployment turns into overemployment. As time goes on, the economy approaches a new long-run equilibrium. All workers again find a job. Firms do not invest, so the stock of capital does not change. In other words, the steady state after disturbance is identical to the steady state before disturbance.

In summary, the investment shock induces a cyclical process of adjustment. What is more, the long-run equilibrium proves to be stable.

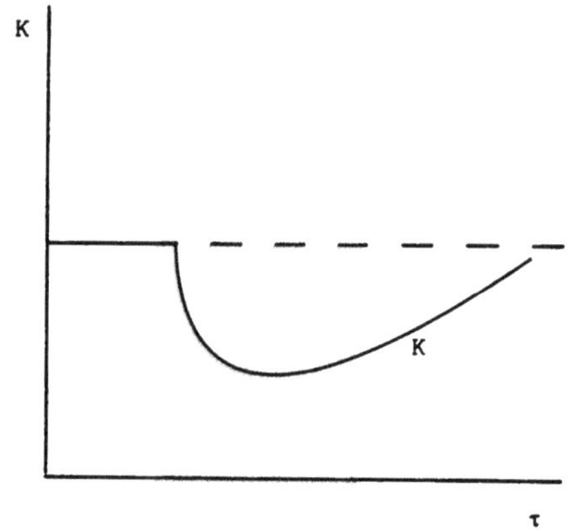

Figure 3. Cyclical Path of Capital Stock.

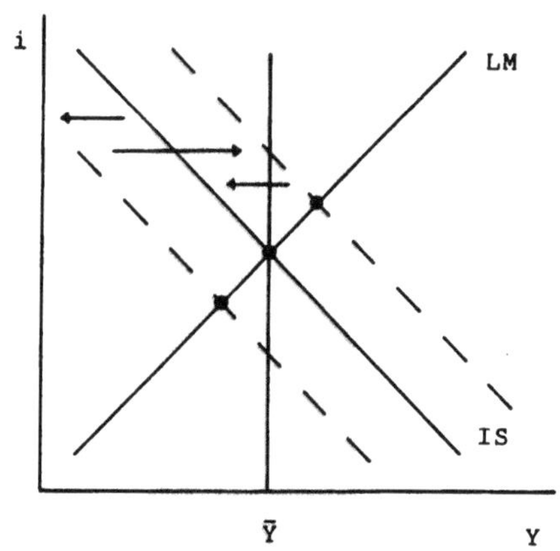

Figure 4. Investment Shock and Cyclical Adjustment.

5.2. Economy With Public Sector

In the current section, we shall suppose that the government runs a passive fiscal policy. That is to say, the government alters neither the tax rate nor public consumption. To begin with, in section 5.2.1., the analysis will be implemented within the overlapping generations model.There, the focus will be on the long-run equilibrium. Then, in section 5.2.2., we shall inaugurate the multiplier-accelerator model. In that place, emphasis will be laid on the process of adjustment. Last but not least, the two approaches will be connected.

5.2.1. Overlapping Generations Model

The long-run equilibrium can be characterized by a system of three equations, confer (20) until (23) in section 3.1.:

(1) $$Y = K^{\alpha} N^{\beta}$$

(2) $$K = \beta\delta(1-t)Y$$

(3) $$G = tY$$

Without loss of generality, we postulate that at the start there is no public debt $D=0$. Here, α, β, δ, G and N are given exogenously, whereas t, K and Y are endogenous variables. The number of equations matches the number of unknowns, so the system can be solved. In the stationary equilibrium, full employment prevails. Labour demand, the stock of capital and output are constant. Firms abstain from investment $I=0$. Besides, households and the government consume the whole of income $C+G=Y$.

Initially, the economy is in the long-run equilibrium. Then, abruptly, an investment shock occurs, which turns out to be transitory. Sales expectations deteriorate, at least for the moment. As time proceeds, the economy gravitates to a new long-run equilibrium. The post-shock steady-state is the same as the pre-shock steady-state, because no parameter of the model has been affected. During the process of adjustment, nothing happens. This can be ascribed to the fact that, within this context, firms have no difficulty to sell their output. But as far as the short run is concerned, this premise seems to be rather unrealistic.

5.2.2. Multiplier-Accelerator Model

Let us begin with the short-run equilibrium. Firms produce as much as households, firms and the government want to buy $Y=C+I+G$. Public consumption is assumed to be fixed $G=\bar{G}=\text{const}$. In addition, the government levies an income tax $T=tY$ at the flat rate $t=\text{const}$. The budget deficit is defined as the excess of public spending over tax revenue $B=G-T$ or $B=G-tY$. Over time, government borrowing augments public debt $D_{+1}=D+B$.

Obviously, the interest payments on public debt have not been included into the analysis. This can be justified on the following grounds: At the outset, no public debt does exist. During the process of adjustment, public debt remains small. And ultimately, public debt will be retired altogether. Admittedly, this argument is somewhat circular, therefore this point will be resumed in chapter 6.

Factor income net after tax constitutes disposable income $Y_d=Y-T$ or $Y_d=(1-t)Y$. Private consumption is a linear function of disposable income $C=\bar{C}+c(1-t)Y$. Private investment serves to fill the gap between the desired stock of capital and the actual stock of capital $I=\lambda(K^*-K)$. The desired stock of capital in turn corresponds to expected sales multiplied by the capital-output ratio $K^*=vE$. Actual sales last period yield expected sales this period $E=Y_{-1}$.

Further, private investment builds up the actual stock of capital round by round $K_{+1} = K + I$.

In full analogy to section 5.1.2., the short-run equilibrium can be represented by a system of nine equations.

(1) $$Y = C + I + G$$

(2) $$C = \bar{C} + c(1-t)Y$$

(3) $$I = \lambda(K^* - K)$$

(4) $$K^* = vE$$

(5) $$E = Y_{-1}$$

(6) $$K_{+1} = K + I$$

(7) $$G = \bar{G}$$

(8) $$B = G - tY$$

(9) $$D_{+1} = D + B$$

At this stage, we leave the short-run equilibrium and turn to the long-run equilibrium. What is the asymptote of this process? In the steady state, the stock of capital does no longer move $K_{+1} = K$. Insert this into (6) to obtain:

(10) $$I = 0$$

That means, firms dispense with investment. Likewise, in the steady state, public debt does no longer vary $D_{+1} = D$. From this together with (9) one can deduce:

(11) $$B = 0$$

Put another way, the budget is balanced. Besides, from (8) and (11) it can be inferred that public consumption agrees with tax revenue $\bar{G} = tY$.

Moreover, substitute (2), (7) and (10) into (1), observing $\bar{G} = tY$, to arrive at:

(12) $$Y = \frac{\bar{C}}{1-c} + \bar{G}$$

Evidently, the stationary level of income is independent of sales expectations. Next eliminate Y_{-1} in (5) with the help of $Y = Y_{-1}$ to get $E = Y$ or

(13) $$E = \frac{\bar{C}}{1-c} + \bar{G}$$

In addition, put (10) into (3) and rearrange: $K^* = K$. Taking account of this and $E = Y$, (4) can be expressed as $K = vY$ or

(14) $$K = \frac{v\bar{C}}{1-c} + v\bar{G}$$

The technology exhibits fixed coefficients:

$$Y = \min\left(\frac{K}{v}, \frac{\bar{N}}{a}\right) \tag{15}$$

As far as the production function is binding, it will do so only in a soft way.

We assume that in the long-run equilibrium before disturbance all workers have got a job $Y = \bar{N}/a$. Now compare this with (12) to reach:

$$\frac{\bar{C}}{1-c} + \bar{G} = \frac{\bar{N}}{a} \tag{16}$$

Let this condition be satisfied. Without losing generality, we posit that in the pre-shock steady state there is no public debt $D = 0$. Then solve $\bar{G} = tY$ for t and eliminate Y by making use of (12):

$$t = \frac{(1-c)\bar{G}}{\bar{C} + (1-c)\bar{G}} \tag{17}$$

Suppose that this condition is met, too.

At the beginning, the economy is in the long-run equilibrium. Then, suddenly, an investment shock takes place. More precisely, expected sales come down. As time goes on, the economy converges to a new long-run equilibrium. The stationary equilibrium after disturbance coincides with the stationary equilibrium before disturbance, as has been demonstrated above. At the end, output, the stock of capital and labour demand return to their original values. Again, all workers find a job. The deeper reason is that all parameters are constant and that expected sales adapt themselves.

Next have a look at the development of public debt over the process of adjustment. First take differences of (8) to achieve $\Delta B = -t\Delta Y$. After that take the sum over all periods of the process $\Sigma \Delta B = -t\Sigma \Delta Y$. By virtue of $\Sigma \Delta Y = 0$, this simplifies to $\Sigma \Delta B = 0$. As a consequence, public debt comes back to its original level. If the initial value of public debt is zero, then the terminal value is also zero. In the long run, public debt does again disappear.

To conclude, what is the relationship beteween the overlapping generations model and the multiplier-accelerator model? We start from the assumption that the two models agree in the pre-shock steady state. Then, as a result, they agree in the post-shock steady state as well. In this sense, the two models harmonize. Here, the multiplier-accelerator model elaborates the process of adjustment. Put differently, money wages and prices need not to accommodate.

5.2.3. Simulation

In the current section, we shall simulate the process of adjustment being set off by an investment shock. Table 9 displays how the economy evolves over time when the government pursues a passive fiscal policy. The numerical example relies on the following parameter values: $c=0.625$, $t=0.2$, $\bar{C}=30$, $\bar{G}=20$, $v=1$, $\lambda=0.2$, $a=1$, and $\bar{N}=100$. The parameter values have been modified so as to keep the multiplier at 2. This specification allows one to trace the time path without much difficulty. In the steady state, output, the stock of capital and labour demand equal 100. This can easily be seen: $Y=(\bar{C}+\bar{G})/[1-c(1-t)]=100$, $K=vY=100$ and $N=aY=100$. In the stationary equilibrium, evidently, full employment prevails.

At the start, in period 0, the economy is in the long-run equilibrium. Businesses put in 100 machines and 100 labourers to fabricate 100 units. All workers have got a job. Private and public consumption add up to income $C+G=100$. Firms refrain from investment $I=0$. Government expenditures are entirely covered by tax revenue $T=G$. The budget is balanced $B=0$, and no public debt does exist $D=0$.

Under these circumstances, in period 1, an investment shock comes about. Strictly speaking, expected sales decline spontaneously from 100 to 90. Therefore, enterprises reduce the planned stock of capital from 100 to 90, too. The actual stock of capital, on the other hand, has already been decided on in period 0. Thus, the desired stock of capital falls short of the actual stock of capital by 10. According to the speed of adjustment 0.2, private investment drops from 0 to -2. With a multiplier of 2, firms contract output from 100 to 96. As a consequence, unemployment arises. The diminution in income goes along with a diminution in tax earnings. More exactly, taxes are cut down from 20 to 19.2. But government purchases stay put at the given level of 20. This brings the budget into a deficit of 0.8.

At this juncture, we close period 1 and open up period 2. The variation in output motivates firms to revise expected sales upwards from 90 to 96. Analogously, the desired stock of capital increases from 90 to 96. The actual stock of capital, however, diminishes from 100 to 98, due to negative investment. Corresponding to the accelerator, private investment is stepped up from -2 to -0.4. As a response, firms expand output from 96 to 99.2. This is being accompanied by a tax rise from 19.2 to 19.8. Public consumption remaining at 20, the budget deficit falls from 0.8 to 0.2. Owing to the budget deficit of the previous period, public debt comes into existence $D=0.8$.

Once again, in period 3, expected sales are corrected upwards, in this instance from 96 to 99.2. Likewise, businesses raise the optimal stock of capital from 96 to 99.2, as opposed to the actual stock of capital, which is lowered from 98 to 97.6. The net effect is to enhance private investment from -0.4 to $+0.3$. In other words, net investment becomes positive. That is why enterprises propel output from 99.2 to 100.6. By the same token, the economy now suffers from overemployment. Tax proceeds improve from 19.8 to 20.1, while government purchases hold fast. On that account, the budget deficit of 0.2 turns into a budget

Table 9

Investment Shock and Passive Fiscal Policy

τ	E	K^*	K	I	Y	G	T	B	D
0	100	100	100	0	100	20	20	0	0
1	90	90	100	- 2	96	20	19.2	0.8	0
2	96	96	98	- 0.4	99.2	20	19.8	0.2	0.8
3	99.2	99.2	97.6	0.3	100.6	20	20.1	- 0.1	1.0
4	100.6	100.6	97.9	0.5	101.1	20	20.2	- 0.2	0.9
5	101.1	101.1	98.4	0.5	101.1	20	20.2	- 0.2	0.7
6	101.1	101.1	98.9	0.4	100.9	20	20.2	- 0.2	0.5
7	100.9	100.9	99.3	0.3	100.6	20	20.1	- 0.1	0.3
8	100.6	100.6	99.6	0.2	100.4	20	20.1	- 0.1	0.2
9	100.4	100.4	99.8	0.1	100.2	20	20	0	0.1
10	100.2	100.2	99.9	0.1	100.1	20	20	0	0.1
11	100.1	100.1	100	0	100	20	20	0	0
12	100	100	100	0	100	20	20	0	0

surplus of 0.1. Besides, public borrowing of the last period builds up public debt from 0.8 to 1.0.

This process recurs round by round. At the end, in period 12, firms again employ 100 machines and 100 workers to manufacture 100 units. The labour market clears once more. Households and the government buy the whole of production. Enterprises do no longer invest. Tax revenue matches public consumption, the budget is balanced, and public debt has evaporated. That means, the economy returns to a long-run equilibrium. What is more, the terminal steady state coincides with the initial steady state.

Figure 1 plots the cyclical path of output. At the outset, firms operate at the full-employment level. Then, abruptly, the investment shock drives down output. With the lapse of time, firms elevate output, at a certain date passing the full-employment level. Eventually, production settles down at its original value. Similarly, figure 2 graphs the budget balance across the cycle. At the beginning, let there be no public debt at all. Then, because of the disturbance, the budget at first gets into deficit and later on into surplus. Therefore, public debt rises, reaches a maximum and finally falls off.

Properly speaking, the process of adjustment can be split up into two stages, confer figure 3. Initially, the economy is in the long-run equilibrium. All workers have got a job. Firms abstain from investment, so the stock of capital does not change. The budget is balanced, and no public debt does exist. In figure 3, the common point of intersection of the IS schedule, the LM schedule, the $\bar{Y}$ vertical and the GT line marks the stationary state.

Then, in the first stage, sales expectations deteriorate exogenously. On that ground, businesses defer the replacement of capital. In figure 3, correspondingly, the IS schedule shifts to the left. Firms have to lay off workers, so unemployment emerges. Private investment becomes negative, thereby decumu-

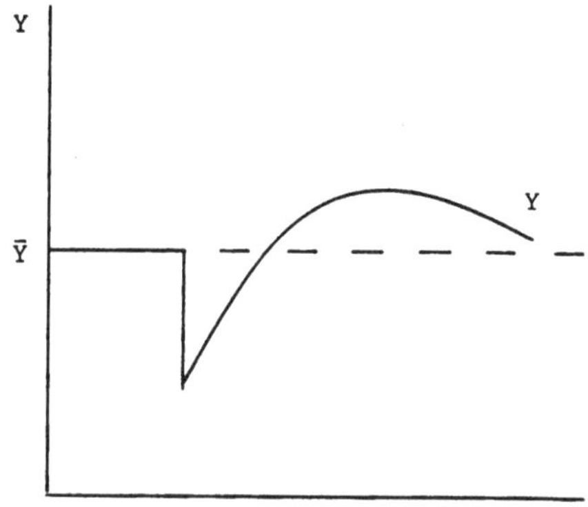

Figure 1. Output Cycle.

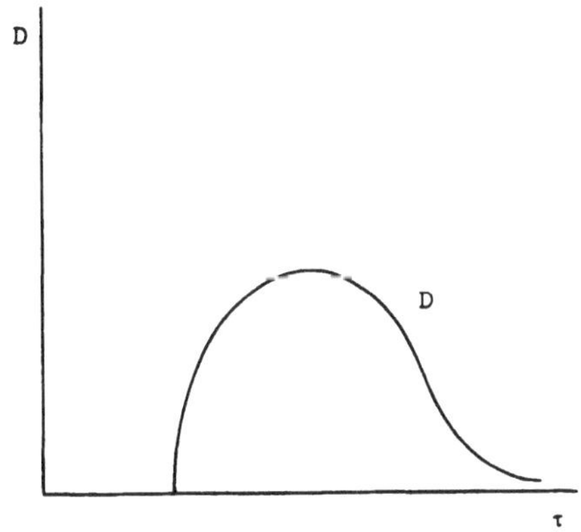

Figure 2. Cyclical Budget Balance.

lating capital. The reduction in income calls forth a reduction in taxes. This brings the budget into deficit, hence public debt grows round by round.

In the second stage, sales expectations recover endogenously. As a response, enterprises make up for the replacement of capital. Accordingly, the IS schedule sharply moves to the right, thus shooting over its original position. Firms try to engage additional workers to such an extent that labour demand exceeds supply. Investment becomes positive, so capital is being replenished. Further, the increase in income leads to an increase in taxes. Now the budget shows a surplus, hence public debt declines.

Ultimately, the economy tends to a new long-run equilibrium. Again, all workers find a job. Firms do no longer invest, so the stock of capital is invariant.

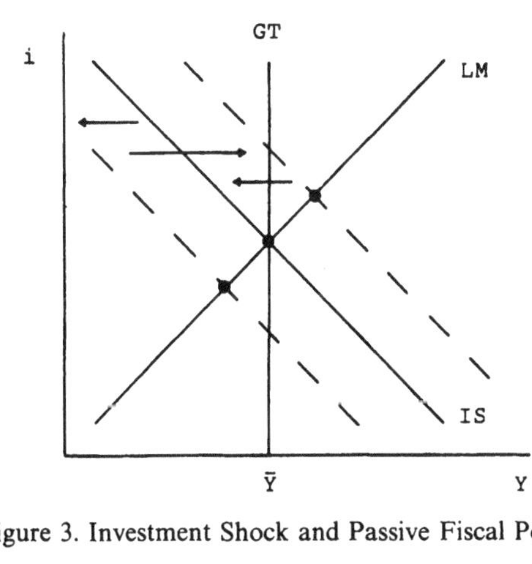

Figure 3. Investment Shock and Passive Fiscal Policy.

The budget is balanced, and public debt has been paid off completely. By the way, the post-shock steady state is identical to the pre-shock steady state.

In summary, the investment shock generates a cyclical process of adjustment. What is more, the long-run equilibrium proves to be stable. As a fundamental result, the budget will be balanced over the cycle.

Last but not least, how does the economy with public sector perform as compared to the economy without public sector? The answer is that the presence of government activities lowers the variation of income. Unfortunately, this does not become clear in the current section. This can be attributed to the fact that we raised the marginal propensity to consume from 0.5 to 0.625 in order to maintain the multiplier at 2 for expository purposes.

5.3. Economy With Fiscal Policy

In the present section, we shall assume that the government runs an active fiscal policy. Strictly speaking, the government adapts public consumption so as to secure full employment. The tax rate, on the other hand, remains unchanged.

The current section is organized as follows. To begin with, in section 5.3.1., we shall briefly recall the overlapping generations model. There, the accent will be put on the long-run equilibrium. Then, in section 5.3.2., we shall discuss the multiplier-accelerator model. In that place, the process of adjustment will be studied in more depth. Finally, we shall tie up these two modes of analysis.

5.3.1. Overlapping Generations Model

In the same way as in section 3.1., the long-run equilibrium can be described by a system of three equations:

(1) $$Y = K^{\alpha} N^{\beta}$$

(2) $$K = \beta\delta(1-t)Y$$

(3) $$G = tY$$

At the outset, let there be no public debt $D=0$. Hence public consumption equals tax revenue. Here, α, β, δ, G and N are given exogenously, while t, K and Y are endogenous variables. The number of equations matches the number of unknowns, so the system is well defined. In the steady state, the labour market clears. Labour supply, the stock of capital and output are constant. Firms abstain from investment $I=0$. Households and the government take in the whole of output $C+G=Y$.

Initially, the economy is in the long-run equilibrium. Then an investment shock comes about, since sales expectations deteriorate. Over time, the economy converges to a new long-run equilibrium. The steady state after disturbance coincides with the steady state before disturbance, as no parameter of the model has been touched. During the process of adjustment, nothing happens. This can be attributed to the premise that firms have no problem to merchandise their output. In the short term, however, this premise appears to be somewhat delusive.

5.3.2. Multiplier-Accelerator Model

For ease of exposition, the money market will still be excluded from the analysis. At first we shall deal with the short-run equilibrium and after that with the long-run equilibrium.

Let us start with the short-run equilibrium. We suppose here that the government pursues an active fiscal policy. More precisely, the government accommodates public consumption G so as to keep up full employment $Y=\bar{Y}$. Further, the government collects an income tax $T=t\bar{Y}$ at the flat rate $t=$const. The budget deficit is given by the difference between public spending and tax proceeds $B=G-T=G-t\bar{Y}$. The budget deficit adds to public debt round by round $D_{+1}=D+B$. Tacitly, public interest has been disregarded at the present stage. At the beginning, no public debt does exist. During the process of adjustment, public debt remains only small. And ultimately, it will completely be retired.

Factor income, diminished by taxation, yields disposable income: $Y_d=\bar{Y}-T=(1-t)\bar{Y}$. Private consumption is a linear function of disposable income: $C=\bar{C}+c(1-t)\bar{Y}$. At this point, it is useful to return to public consumption. The government alters public expenditures such that full employment is maintained $Y=\bar{Y}$, as has been mentioned above. Output can be devoted to private consumption, private investment and public consumption $\bar{Y}=C+I+G$. Now insert the consumption function to arrive at $\bar{Y}=\bar{C}+c(1-t)\bar{Y}+I+G$. From this one can deduce the required level of government purchases $G=\bar{G}-I$, where $\bar{G}$ stands for the steady-state level of public consumption.

Private investment serves to close the gap between the desired stock of capital and the actual stock of capital step by step $I=\lambda(K^*-K)$. The desired stock of capital in turn is the product of expected sales and the capital-output ratio $K^*=vE$. Expected sales correspond to full-employment output $E=\bar{Y}$, as opposed to the case considered before. Naturally, private investment augments the stock of capital $K_{+1}=K+I$.

In summary, the short-run equilibrium can be represented by a system of nine equations:

(1) $$\bar{Y}=C+I+G$$

(2) $$C=\bar{C}+c(1-t)\bar{Y}$$

(3) $$I=\lambda(K^*-K)$$

(4) $$K^* = vE$$

(5) $$E = \bar{Y}$$

(6) $$K_{+1} = K + I$$

(7) $$G = \bar{G} - I$$

(8) $$B = G - t\bar{Y}$$

(9) $$D_{+1} = D + B$$

The next point refers to the long-run equilibrium. In the steady state, the stock of capital does not move $K_{+1} = K$. Substitute this into (6) to see that firms do no longer invest:

(10) $$I = 0$$

Now combine (3) with (10) to get $K^* = K$. Then put this into (4), paying attention to (5):

(11) $$K = v\bar{Y}$$

In the steady state, public debt does neither accumulate nor decumulate $D_{+1} = D$. From this together with (9) one can infer that the budget will be balanced:

(12) $$B = 0$$

Finally, eliminate B and G in (8) with the help of (12) and $G = \bar{G}$ to reach $\bar{G} = t\bar{Y}$.

The production function is characterized by fixed coefficients:

(13) $$Y = \min\left(\frac{K}{v}, \frac{\bar{N}}{a}\right)$$

If the resource constraint is binding, it will do so only in a soft way.

We postulate that in the long-run equilibrium before disturbance there is no public debt $D = 0$, which involves $\bar{G} = t\bar{Y}$. Moreover, we posit that full employment prevails in the pre-shock steady state $\bar{Y} = \bar{N}/a$. Now insert (2), (10) as well as $G = \bar{G} = t\bar{Y}$ into (1) and solve for $\bar{Y}$:

(14) $$\bar{Y} = \frac{\bar{C} + \bar{G}}{1 - c}$$

We assume that this condition is fulfilled. Besides, solve $\bar{G} = t\bar{Y}$ for t, observing (14):

(15) $$t = \frac{(1-c)\bar{G}}{\bar{C} + (1-c)\bar{G}}$$

Let this requirement also be met.

At the outset, the economy is in the long-run equilibrium. In this situation, abruptly, sales expectations worsen. In order to prevent unemployment from coming into existence, the government switches over to a fiscal expansion. In due course, the economy approaches a new long-run equilibrium. Over and above that, the post-shock steady state is identical to the pre-shock steady state. Especially, the stock of capital returns to its original value. The reason is that all parameters of the model are constant and that sales expectations improve themselves.

What does this mean for public debt? First take differences of $B = G - tY$, noting $\Delta Y = 0$, to obtain $\Delta B = \Delta G$. Then sum over all periods $\Sigma \Delta B = \Sigma \Delta G$. By virtue of $\Sigma \Delta G = 0$, this implies $\Sigma \Delta B = 0$. That is to say, the sum over all budget deficits is zero. In other words, if the initial value of public debt amounts to zero, then the terminal value will be equal to zero, too. At the end, public debt will entirely be redeemed.

Last but not least, we shall attempt to combine the overlapping generations model and the multiplier-accelerator model. We start from the premise that the two models agree in the pre-shock steady state. Then, as a consequence, they agree in the post-shock steady state as well. In this sense, the two models amalgamate, the multiplier-accelerator model being primarily concerned with the process of adjustment. Put differently money wages and prices need not to change.

5.3.3. Simulation

In the current section we shall compute the process of adjustment being set in motion by an investment shock. Table 10 permits to track the time path under an active fiscal policy. The numerical example will be based on the following parameter values: $c = 0.625$, $t = 0.2$, $\bar{C} = 30$, $\bar{G} = 20$, $v = 1$, $\lambda = 0.2$, $a = 1$ and $\bar{N} = 100$. In the long term, this provides $Y = (\bar{C} + \bar{G})/[1 - c(1-t)] = 100$, $K = vY = 100$ and $N = aY = 100$. In other words, there will be full employment.

At the beginning, in period 0, the economy is in the long run equilibrium. Firms produce 100 units by making use of 100 machines and 100 workers. Therefore, the labour market clears. Households and the government exhaust the whole of income $C + G = 100$. Businesses refrain from investment $I = 0$. Government purchases are financed by tax receipts $T = G$, so the budget is balanced $B = 0$. Initially, let there be no public debt $D = 0$.

Against this background, in period 1, an investment shock occurs. More precisely, expected sales fall from 100 to 90. For that reason, enterprises also revise the desired stock of capital from 100 to 90. The actual stock of capital, by way of contrast, has been inherited from the past. According to the speed of adjustment, private investment drops from 0 to -2. In order to avoid unemployment, the government answers by a loose fiscal policy. Properly speaking, the government raises public consumption from 20 to 22, thus filling the gap in aggregate demand. As a result, output does not vary, hence firms still engage all workers. Tax proceeds are constant, since income remains unchanged.

Table 10
Investment Shock and Active Fiscal Policy

t	E	K*	K	I	G	Y	T	B	D
0	100	100	100	0	20	100	20	0	0
1	90	90	100	− 2	22	100	20	2	0
2	100	100	98	0.4	19.6	100	20	− 0.4	2
3	100	100	98.4	0.3	19.7	100	20	− 0.3	1.6
4	100	100	98.7	0.3	19.7	100	20	− 0.3	1.3
5	100	100	99.0	0.2	19.8	100	20	− 0.2	1.0
6	100	100	99.2	0.2	19.8	100	20	− 0.2	0.8
7	100	100	99.4	0.1	19.9	100	20	− 0.1	0.6
8	100	100	99.5	0.1	19.9	100	20	− 0.1	0.5
9	100	100	99.6	0.1	19.9	100	20	− 0.1	0.4
10	100	100	99.7	0.1	19.9	100	20	− 0.1	0.3
11	100	100	99.8	0	20	100	20	0	0.2
∞	100	100	100	0	20	100	20	0	0

In addition, the increase in government expenditures gives rise to a budget deficit of 2.

At this juncture, we leave period 1 and enter period 2. Expected sales return to their original level of 100, because actual sales did not move at all. As a reply, businesses correct the desired stock of capital from 90 to 100, too. The actual stock of capital, on the other hand, declines from 100 to 98, due to the disinvestment undertaken in period 1. On account of this, enterprises boost investment from -2 to $+0.4$. In order to prevent overemployment, the government switches from expansion to contraction. More exactly, the government lowers public consumption from 22 to 19.6, thereby absorbing the excess of aggregate demand. As a consequence, production stays put, so full employment is preserved. This process has no influence on tax revenue, as income remains unaffected. Further, the reduction in government spending brings the budget from deficit into surplus $B=-0.4$. Over and above that, public debt comes into existence $D=2$, owing to the budget deficit in the preceding period.

As time passes by, the economy tends to a new long-run equilibrium ($\tau \rightarrow \infty$). Firms do no longer invest, so the stock of capital is uniform. Besides, the budget is balanced, hence public debt does neither build up nor down. Strictly speaking, public debt comes back to its starting point $D=0$. In addition, the labour market still clears. What is more, the terminal equilibrium is identical to the initial equilibrium.

Figure 1 illustrates the constant time path of output when the government adheres to an active fiscal policy. The trajectory of public debt under active fiscal policy resembles the locus derived under passive fiscal policy, see figure 2 in section 5.2.3.

The process of adjustment once more consists of two phases, compare figure 2. At the beginning, the economy is in the stationary equilibrium. Specifically, all

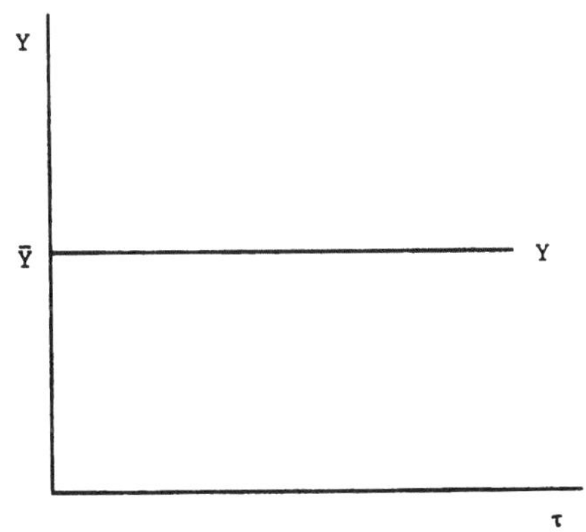

Figure 1. Time Path of Output.

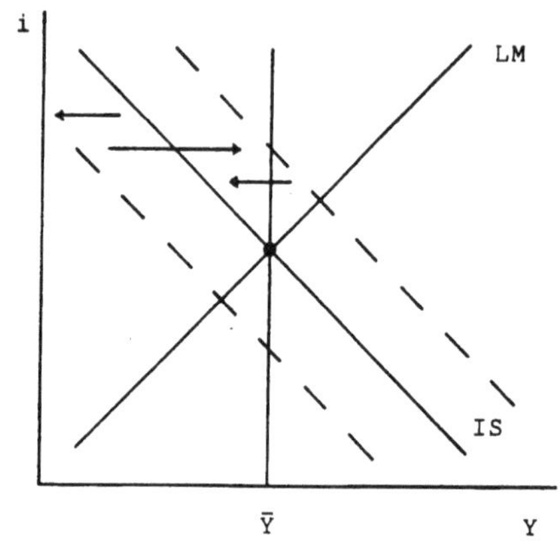

Figure 2. Investment Shock and Active Fiscal Policy.

workers have got a job. Firms dispense with investment, so the stock of capital does not change. The budget is balanced, and no public debt does exist. In the diagram, the original steady state lies in the intersection of the IS schedule, the LM schedule and the $\bar{Y}$ vertical.

During the first phase, sales expectations deteriorate exogenously. On that ground, businesses put off the replacement of capital. Accordingly, the IS curve moves to the left. Private investment becomes negative, thus the stock of capital declines. In order to reestablish full employment, the government raises public consumption. In figure 2, the IS curve shifts to the right, returning into its initial position. The budget gets into deficit, thereby accumulating public debt.

During the second phase, sales expectations recover endogenously. This encourages enterprises to make good the replacement of capital. As a consequence, the IS curve goes to the right. Now private investment turns positive, so the stock of capital grows step by step. In order to restore full employment, the government lowers public expenditures. In the diagram, the IS curve travels back to the left. This brings the budget into surplus, thus paying off public debt round by round.

Ultimately, the economy gravitates to a new stationary equilibrium. All workers still find a job. Firms do no longer invest, so the stock of capital is invariant. The budget is again balanced, and public debt has disappeared from the scence. That is to say, the steady state after disturbance coincides with the steady state before disturbance.

In summary, the investment shock induces a cyclical process of adjustment. This, in turn, requires a cyclical path of fiscal policy. As a major result, the budget will be balanced across the cycle. Over and above that, the long-run equilibrium proves to be stable.

Under active fiscal policy, full employment always prevails. Hence one might object here hat there is no reason why sales expectations should worsen at all. In answering this question, we have to keep in mind that so far time lags have been neglected, mainly to keep matters simple. In the real world, of course, government responds only slowly. When expected sales come down, then actual sales will come down, too. Now it takes a lot of time to recognize the depression and to decide on suitable action. Even more time is needed for the fiscal expansion to work out. Nevertheless, it holds true that policy expectations stabilize prospective sales to a certain degree.

Another problem is associated with the fact of life that goods are heterogenous, differing from industry to industry. An investment shock means that firms buy less capital goods. And a loose fiscal policy, as a reaction, signifies that the government purchases more public goods. Here the question arises whether the capital goods industry is indeed able to produce more public goods. If the reply to this question is yes, then fiscal policy is completely effective.

But if the answer is no, then the multiplier process will enter the stage. In the first round, firms buy less capital goods, thus reducing income. Therefore in the second round, households shop less consumer goods. In order to stimulate aggregate demand, the government tries to spend more on public goods. Now everything depends on whether the consumer goods industry is able to manufacture more public goods. If yes, then fiscal policy is effective at least in part.If no, the government should rather lower the income tax instead of raising public consumption. As a consequence, private agents will market more consumer goods. In this sense, fiscal policy turns out to be partially effective. By the way, the effectiveness is enhanced by the circumstance that overemployment is feasible for some time.

To conclude, how does the economy with fiscal policy perform as compared to the economy with public sector that has been addressed in section 5.2.? The comparative evaluation reveals that the active fiscal policy reduces the fluctuations in investment and capital by more than did the passive fiscal policy. Further, the active fiscal policy drives the variation in income and employment down to zero.

5.4. Alternative Paths

Under different parameter values, the investment shock generates time paths which may well differ in type, as can be learned from simulation experiments. To begin with, in section 5.4.1., a few words will be said on stability. Then, in section 5.4.2., we shall investigate damped oscillations. Finally, in section 5.4.3., we shall take a look at the case of explosive oscillations. There, the focus will be on the role played by fiscal policy.

5.4.1. Stability

In the current section, we shall explore the stability of the long-run equilibrium. Here, the analysis will be restricted to an economy without public sector. At first take differences of $Y = \bar{C} + cY + I$, $I = \lambda(K^* - K)$ and $K^* = vE$, confer (1) until (4) in section 5.1.2. This operation yields $\Delta Y = 1/(1-c)\Delta I$ and $\Delta I = \lambda v \, \Delta E$. Then eliminate ΔI to arrive at:

$$\Delta Y = \frac{\lambda v}{1-c} \Delta E \tag{1}$$

Equation (1) indicates how actual sales respond to expected sales.

This raises the issue under what condition the increase in actual sales will fall short of the increase in expected sales. The evaluation of the multiplier in (1) provides the critical speed of adjustment:

$$\lambda' = \frac{1-c}{v} \tag{2}$$

If $\lambda \lesseqgtr \lambda'$, then $\Delta Y \lesseqgtr \Delta E$, respectively. Put differently, when the stock of capital is adapted slowly, the long-run equilibrium will be stable. Conversely, when the stock of capital accommodates quickly, the long-run equilibrium will be unstable. To illustrate this, consider a numerical example with $c = 0.5$ and $v = 1$, so the critical speed amounts to $\lambda' = 0.5$. If the capital gap is closed by less than half, the process will be damped. On the other hand, if the capital gap is filled by more, the market will explode.

So far, it was convenient to suppose that expected sales this period are determined by actual sales last period. Now, when the adjustment of expectations is subject to a distributed lag, stability becomes even more likely.

5.4.2. Damped Oscillations

In the current section, we shall simulate the process of adjustment triggered by an investment shock. Here, the speed of adjustment is assumed to be $\lambda = 0.4$, so the long-run equilibrium will be stable. In the first step, we shall consider an economy without public sector. Then, in the second step, the government will enter the picture. Finally, in the third step, we shall examine the consequences of an active fiscal policy.

To begin with, we shall address an economy without public sector. Table 11 displays how the economy evolves over time. The calculations rely on the following parameter values: $c = 0.5$, $\bar{C} = 50$, $v = 1$, $a = 1$ and $\bar{N} = 100$.

Initially, in period 0, the economy is in the steady state, reproducing itself. Firms manufacture 100 units with the help of 100 machines and 100 workers. Full employment prevails. Households take in the whole of output, while firms abstain from investment altogether. In this situation, in period 1, an investment shock emerges. More precisely, expected sales come down from 100 to 90. This sets in motion a drawn-out process of adjustment, which ultimately brings the economy back to the original steady state.

As a result, the investment shock leads to damped oscillations, see figure 1. In other words, the long-run equilibrium proves to be stable.

Next, the public sector will be introduced into the model. Table 12 presents a synopsis of the process of adjustment when the government runs a passive fiscal policy. The simulation will be based on the subsequent parameter values: $c=0.625$, $t=0.2$, $\bar{C}=30$, $\bar{G}=20$, $v=1$, $a=1$ and $\bar{N}=100$.

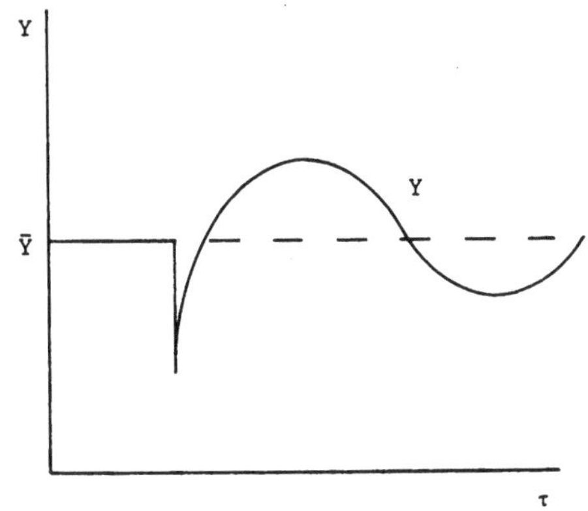

Figure 1. Investment Shock and Damped Oscillations.

At the start, in period 0, the economy is in the stationary equilibrium. All workers have got a job. Households and the government entirely consume income $C+G=100$. Firms refrain from investment $I=0$. Tax proceeds exactly match public consumption $T=G$, hence the budget is balanced $B=0$. At the outset, let there be no public debt $D=0$. Against this background, in period 1, an investment shock occurs. Strictly speaking, sales expectations deteriorate from 100 to 90. Eventually, for $\tau\rightarrow\infty$, the economy returns to the initial equilibrium without public debt.

To summarize, the investment shock again causes damped oscillations. That is to say, the stationary equilibrium turns out to be stable. What is more, the budget will be balanced over the oscillations taken together.

Last but not least, we shall postulate that the government pursues an active fiscal policy. That means, the government varies public consumption in such a way as to maintain full employment. Accordingly, table 13 gives an overview of the resulting time path.

Table 11

Investment Shock and Damped Oscillations ($\lambda = 0.4$)

τ	E	K^*	K	I	Y
0	100	100	100	0	100
1	90	90	100	− 4	92
2	92	92	96	− 1,6	96.8
3	96.8	96.8	94.4	1.0	101.9
4	101.9	101.9	95.4	2.6	105.2
5	105.2	105.2	98.0	2.9	105.8
6	105.8	105.8	100.9	2.0	103.9
7	103.9	103.9	102.9	0.4	100.8
8	100.8	100.8	103.3	− 1.0	98.0
9	98.0	98.0	102.3	− 1.7	96.6
10	96.6	96.6	100.6	− 1.6	96.8
11	96.8	96.8	99.0	− 0.9	98.2
12	98.2	98.2	98.1	0.0	100.0
13	100.0	100.0	98.1	0.8	101.5
∞	100	100	100	0	100

Table 12

Investment Shock and Passive Fiscal Policy ($\lambda = 0.4$)

τ	E	K*	K	I	Y	G	T	B	D
0	100	100	100	0	100	20	20	0	0
1	90	90	100	− 4	92	20	18.4	1.6	0
2	92	92	96	− 1.6	96.8	20	19.4	0.6	1.6
3	96.8	96.8	94.4	1.0	101.9	20	20.4	− 0.4	2.2
4	101.9	101.9	95.4	2.6	105.2	20	21.0	− 1.0	1.8
5	105.2	105.2	98.0	2.9	105.8	20	21.2	− 1.2	0.8
6	105.8	105.8	100.9	2.0	103.9	20	20.8	− 0.8	− 0.4
7	103.9	103.9	102.9	0.4	100.8	20	20.2	− 0.2	− 1.2
8	100.8	100.8	103.3	− 1.0	98.0	20	19.6	0.4	− 1.4
9	98.0	98.0	102.3	− 1.7	96.6	20	19.3	0.7	− 1.0
10	96.6	96.6	100.6	− 1.6	96.8	20	19.4	0.6	− 0.3
∞	100	100	100	0	100	20	20	0	0

At the beginning, in period 0, the economy is in the long-run equilibrium. The labour market clears. The budget is balanced, and no public debt does exist. Under these circumstances, in period 1, an investment shock happens: Expected sales drop from 100 to 90. As time goes on, the economy tends to come back to the original equilibrium without public debt.

To conclude, the investment shock generates a cyclical movement of both capital and public debt. More precisely, the damped oscillations are transformed by the active fiscal policy into a half cycle. As a finding, the long-run equilibrium is stable. Over and above that, the budget will be balanced across the cycle.

5.4.3. Explosive Oscillations

In the current section, we shall simulate the process of adjustment started by an investment shock. Here, the speed of adjustment is fixed at $\lambda = 1$, thus the long-run equilibrium will be unstable, as opposed to the preceding section. At first, we shall regard an economy without public sector. Later on, the government will be included into the analysis, running either a passive or an active fiscal policy.

To begin with, have a look at an economy without public sector. Correspondingly, table 14 shows how the economy develops over time.

Initially, in period 0, the economy is in the steady state. Particularly, all workers find a job. Then, in period 1, an investment shock takes place. Expected sales diminish from 100 to 90. As a response, firms cut down output from 100 to 80. In this case, the reduction in actual sales by far exceeds the reduction in expected sales. That is to say, the disturbance gives rise to explosive oscillations. Finally, in period 8, the disturbance drives output down to zero. As a consequence, the economy will break down. Strictly speaking, however, output is also limited by the stock of capital and by labour supply. For instance, in period 4, firms employ 80 machines and 100 workers to fabricate 140 units, which obviously is not feasible.

As a result, the investment shock releases explosive oscillations, compare figure 1. In other words, the steady state proves to be unstable.

Now the government enters the stage. Table 15 illuminates the time path under passive fiscal policy. At the start, in period 0, the economy is in the stationary equilibrium. Specifically, full employment prevails. The budget is balanced, and no public debt does exist. Then, in period 1, an investment shock comes about. Sales expectations worsen from 100 to 90, thereby setting off explosive oscillations. Ultimately, in period 8, the economy will collapse.

In summary, the investment shock induces explosive oscillations. Put differently, the stationary equilibrium turns out to be unstable. What is more, the budget will not be balanced over the oscillations taken together.

Table 13

Investment Shock and Active Fiscal Policy ($\lambda = 0.4$)

τ	E	K^*	K	I	G	Y	T	B	D
0	100	100	100	0	20	100	20	0	0
1	90	90	100	−4	24	100	20	4	0
2	100	100	96	1.6	18.4	100	20	−1.6	4
3	100	100	97.6	1.0	19.0	100	20	−1.0	2.4
4	100	100	98.6	0.6	19.4	100	20	−0.6	1.4
5	100	100	99.2	0.3	19.7	100	20	−0.3	0.8
6	100	100	99.5	0.2	19.8	100	20	−0.2	0.5
7	100	100	99.7	0.1	19.9	100	20	−0.1	0.3
∞	100	100	100	0	20	100	20	0	0

Table 14

Investment Shock and Explosive Oscillations ($\lambda = 1$)

τ	E	K^*	K	I	Y
0	100	100	100	0	100
1	90	90	100	− 10	80
2	80	80	90	− 10	80
3	80	80	80	0	100
4	100	100	80	20	140
5	140	140	100	40	180
6	180	180	140	40	180
7	180	180	180	0	100
8	100	100	180	− 80	0

Table 15

Investment Shock and Passive Fiscal Policy ($\lambda = 1$)

τ	E	K*	K	I	Y	G	T	B	D
0	100	100	100	0	100	20	20	0	0
1	90	90	100	- 10	80	20	16	4	0
2	80	80	90	- 10	80	20	16	4	4
3	80	80	80	0	100	20	20	0	8
4	100	100	80	20	140	20	28	- 8	8
5	140	140	100	40	180	20	36	- 16	0
6	180	180	140	40	180	20	36	- 16	- 16
7	180	180	180	0	100	20	20	0	- 32
8	100	100	180	- 80	0	20	0	20	- 32

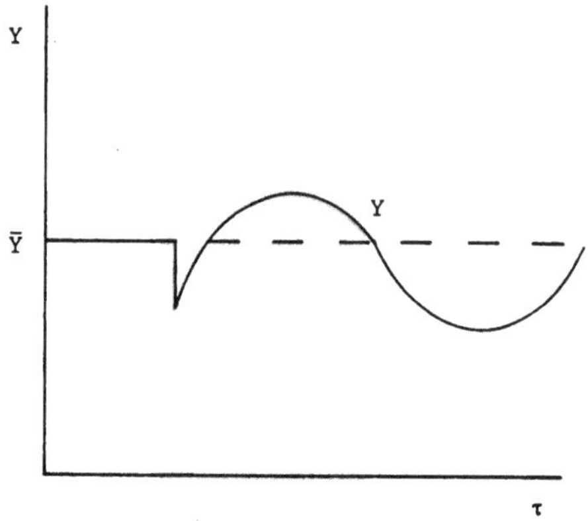

Figure 1. Investment Shock and Explosive Oscillations.

Last but not least, we posit that the government adheres to an active fiscal policy. That means, the government adapts public consumption so as to keep up full employment. Accordingly, table 16 visualizes the ensuing process of adjustment.

Initially, in period 0, the economy moves in the long-run equilibrium. The labour market clears. The budget is balanced, and no public debt does exist. Against this background, in period 1, an investment shock emerges. More precisely, expected sales come down from 100 to 90. For that reason, firms wish to lower investment from 0 to −10. In order to circumvent unemployment, the government raises public consumption from 20 to 30. Therefore, output stays at 100. Further, the budget gets into a deficit of 10.

Then, in period 2, expected sales recover from 90 to 100. On that account, firms want to replenish the stock of capital, hence they push up investment from −10 to +10. To compensate for this, the government pulls down public expenditures from 30 to 10. Thus output still remains at 100. Over and above that, the tight fiscal policy brings the budget into a surplus of 10.

Finally, in period 3, the economy is back in the long-run equilibrium. Firms continue to engage all workers. The budget is again balanced, and public debt has been wiped out. How does the economy with active fiscal policy perform as compared to the economy with passive fiscal policy? Under passive fiscal policy, in period 8, the economy breaks down. Yet under active fiscal policy, in period 3, the economy returns to its original equilibrium.

To sum up, the disturbance causes a cyclical adjustment of both capital and public debt. More exactly, the explosive oscillations are transformed by active fiscal policy into a half cycle. Put another way, the active fiscal policy renders the long-run equilibrium stable. In addition, the budget will be balanced across the cycle.

Table 16
Investment Shock and Active Fiscal Policy ($\lambda = 1$)

τ	0	1	2	3
E	100	90	100	100
K^*	100	90	100	100
K	100	100	90	100
I	0	- 10	10	0
G	20	30	10	20
Y	100	100	100	100
T	20	20	20	20
B	0	10	- 10	0
D	0	0	10	0

6. Investment Shock, Public Interest and Cyclical Adjustment

In the current chapter, public interest will be incorporated into the model. With this exception, we shall take the same avenue as before. The focus will be on the process of adjustment induced by an investment shock. The plan of this chapter goes as follows. To begin with, in section 6.1., we shall consider an economy with public sector. There, the government will run a passive fiscal policy. Instead, in section 6.2., we shall suppose that the government pursues an active fiscal policy. Finally, in section 6.3., we shall discuss stability for the case of a simple economy.

6.1. Economy With Public Sector

In the present section, we shall assume throughout that the government adheres to a passive fiscal policy. Properly speaking, both the tax rate and public consumption are invariant. At first, in section 6.1.1., we shall recall the overlapping generations model. In that place, the long-run equilibrium will be at the center stage. After that, in section 6.1.2., we shall study the multiplier-accelerator model. There, emphasis will be laid on the process of adjustment. Eventually, the two approaches will be linked up.

6.1.1. Overlapping Generations Model

The long-run equilibrium can be compressed into a system of three equations, as is familiar from section 5.2.1. above:

(1) $$Y = K^{\alpha} N^{\beta}$$

(2) $$K = \beta\delta(1-t)\,Y$$

(3) $$G = tY$$

The budget is balanced. At the outset, let there be no public debt, without losing generality. Therefore, public consumption matches tax revenue. Here, α, β, δ, G and N are given exogenously, whereas t, K and Y are endogenous variables. There are as many equations as unknowns, thus the system is definite.

Now, what are the salient features of the long-run equilibrium? Of course, all workers have got a job. Labour supply, the stock of capital and output are fixed. Firms dispense with investment, while households and the government consume the total of income.

Initially, the economy is in the long-run equilibrium. Then, suddenly, an investment shock occurs. Sales expectations deteriorate, thereby disrupting the stationary equilibrium. With the lapse of time, the economy converges to a new long-run equilibrium. Beyond that, the post-shock steady state coincides with the pre-shock steady state, since no parameter of the model has been affected. During the process of adjustment, nothing happens. This can be ascribed to the fact that firms have no problem to sell their output. In the short run, however, this assumption seems to be rather heroic.

6.1.2. Multiplier-Accelerator Model

The augmented multiplier-accelerator model offers the real analysis of a stationary economy. First of all, we shall introduce the short-run equilibrium. Later on, we shall explore the long-run equilibrium.

Let us begin with the short-run equilibrium. Output corresponds to private consumption, private investment and public consumption $Y = C + I + G$. Here, private consumption is a linear function of disposable income $C = \bar{C} + cY_d$.

Moreover, the government buys a certain volume of public goods $G = \bar{G} = \text{const}$. In addition, the government imposes a tax at the flat rate $t = \text{const}$ on both factor income and debt income $T = t(Y + iD)$. For ease of exposition, the rate of interest is assumed to be fixed $i = \text{const}$. The government pays the interest rate i on public debt D, so public interest amounts to iD. The budget deficit is defined as the excess of public consumption and public interest over tax revenue $B = G + iD - T$. Now insert the tax function to reach $B = G + iD - t(Y + iD)$. Public debt plus public borrowing this period provide public debt next period $D_{+1} = D + B$.

Factor income and debt income, net after tax respectively, constitute disposable income $Y_d = Y + iD - T$. Apparently, this expression can be restated as $Y_d = (1-t)(Y + iD)$. Taking account of this, we are able to write private consumption as $C = \bar{C} + c(1-t)(Y + iD)$. Further, private investment serves to fill the gap between the desired stock of capital and the actual stock of capital $I = \lambda(K^* - K)$. The desired stock of capital, in turn, hinges on expected sales $K^* = vE$, where v denotes the capital-output ratio. In the most simple case, expected sales this period are dominated by actual sales last period $E = Y_{-1}$. Evidently, private investment builds up the stock of capital $K_{+1} = K + I$.

In summary, the short-run equilibrium can be described by a system of nine equations:

(1) $$Y = C + I + G$$

(2) $$C = \bar{C} + c(1-t)(Y + iD)$$

(3) $$I = \lambda(K^* - K)$$

(4) $$K^* = vE$$

(5) $$E = Y_{-1}$$

(6) $$K_{+1} = K + I$$

(7) $$G = \bar{G}$$

(8) $$B = G + iD - t(Y + iD)$$

(9) $$D_{+1} = D + B$$

At this point, we leave the short-run equilibrium and turn to the long-run equilibrium. In the steady state, the stock of capital does not move $K_{+1} = K$. Substitute this into (6) to obtain:

(10) $$I = 0$$

That is to say, firms refrain from investment. Besides, in the steady state, public debt does neither accumulate nor decumulate $D_{+1} = D$. Put this into (9) to arrive at:

(11) $$B = 0$$

In other words, the budget is balanced.

After that, solve (8) for public interest, noting (7) and (11):

(12) $$iD = \frac{tY - \bar{G}}{1 - t}$$

Then eliminate C, I and G in (1) by means of (2), (7) and (10), observing (12):

(13) $$Y = \frac{\bar{C}}{1 - c} + \bar{G}$$

As a consequence, the stationary level of income is independent of both sales expectations and public interest. Incidentally, combine (5) with $Y = Y_{-1}$ to get $E = Y$ or:

(14) $$E = \frac{\bar{C}}{1 - c} + \bar{G}$$

Further, from (3) and (10) one can deduce that $K^* = K$. Finally, insert this together with $E = Y$ into (4):

(15) $$K = \frac{v\bar{C}}{1 - c} + v\bar{G}$$

The technology exhibits fixed coefficients:

$$Y = \min\left(\frac{K}{v}, \frac{\bar{N}}{a}\right) \tag{16}$$

As far as the production function is binding, it will do so in a soft way.

We posit that full employment prevails in the long-run equilibrium before disturbance $Y = \bar{N}/a$. Compare this with (13) to verify:

$$\frac{\bar{C}}{1-c} + \bar{G} = \frac{\bar{N}}{a} \tag{17}$$

Let this condition be satisfied. Moreover, without loss of generality, we start from the premise that no public debt does exist in the long-run equilibrium before disturbance. Thus the budget constraint $\bar{G} + iD = t(Y + iD)$ simplifies to $\bar{G} = tY$. Now solve this for t, paying attention to (13):

$$t = \frac{(1-c)\bar{G}}{\bar{C} + (1-c)\bar{G}} \tag{18}$$

Let this requirement be met, too.

Initially, the economy is in the long-run equilibrium. Then, abruptly, sales expectations worsen, thereby initiating an investment shock. In due course, sales expectations improve again, hence the economy tends to a new long-run equilibrium. Here, the post-shock steady state is identical to the pre-shock steady state. Particularly, output, the stock of capital and employment return to their original position. Ultimately, the labour market clears again. The reason is that all parameters of the model remain unchanged and that sales expectations are adapted appropriately.

What does this mean for the trajectory of public debt? Take the budget constraint $\bar{G} + iD = t(Y + iD)$ as a baseline. The comparative-static analysis reveals that the disturbance does not affect $\bar{G}$, t and Y . Owing to that, $\bar{G} = tY$ is valid in the post-shock steady state as well. This implies $iD = 0$ and $D = 0$. In the long-run equilibrium after disturbance, therefore, public debt will have been effaced.

Coming to an end, we shall link up the overlapping generations model and the multiplier-accelerator model. We assume that the two models agree in the long-run equilibrium before disturbance. Then, as a finding, they also agree in the long-run equilibrium after disturbance. In this sense, the two models accord with one another.

6.1.3. Simulation

So far, we have dealt with the comparative statics. Now we shall address the dynamics. More precisely, we shall simulate the process of adjustment called forth by an investment shock. Table 17 displays how the economy evolves over time, given passive fiscal policy. The numerical example rests on the following parameter values: $c = 0.625$, $t = 0.2$, $\bar{C} = 30$, $\bar{G} = 20$, $v = 1$, $\lambda = 0.2$, $a = 1$, $\bar{N} = 100$ and $i = 0.1$.

At the beginning, in period 0, the economy is in the long-run equilibrium. Firms make use of 100 machines and 100 workers to produce 100 units. All workers have got a job. Households and the government consume the whole of income $C + G = 100$, while firms abstain from investment $I = 0$. At the outset, let there be no public debt $D = 0$. Tax revenue equals public consumption $T = G$, so the budget is balanced $B = 0$.

Under these circumstances, in period 1, an investment shock takes place. Strictly speaking, expected sales drop from 100 to 90. On that ground, firms lower the desired stock of capital from 100 to 90, too. The actual stock of capital, on the other hand, has been decided on in period 0, hence it does not react. Accordingly, firms reduce investment from 0 to -2. Still no public debt does exist, because the budget was balanced in period 0. Correspondingly, public interest amounts to zero.

In the next step, we shall derive the variation in output. Substitute $C = \bar{C} + c(1-t)(Y + iD)$ into $Y = C + I + G$, solve for Y and take differences:

(1) $$\Delta Y = \frac{\Delta I + c(1-t)\,\Delta iD}{1 - c(1-t)}$$

From this one can infer that output falls from 100 to 96. As a consequence, unemployment emerges. The decline in income goes along with a decline in tax earnings from $T = t(Y + iD) = 20$ to 19.2. Yet public consumption stays put at $G = 20$. These effects bring the budget into a deficit of $B = G + iD - t(Y + iD) = 0.8$.

At this point, we close period 1 and open up period 2. Expected sales climb from 90 to 96, by virtue of the experience gained in period 0. Likewise, businesses raise the desired stock of capital from 90 to 96. But the actual stock of capital is run down from 100 to 98, on account of the negative investment done in period 1. As a response, enterprises lift investment from -2 to -0.4. Due to the budget deficit in period 1, public debt comes into existence. The government pays the interest rate 0.1 on public debt 0.8, so public interest amounts to 0.08.

Firms answer by expanding output from 96 to 99.28. The rise in income is accompanied by a rise in tax receipts from 19.2 to 19.87. Yet public consumption holds fast. For that reason, the budget deficit is cut down from 0.8 to 0.21. This process of adjustment repeats itself round by round.

Figure 1 plots the resulting time path. In principle, it reminds one of the conclusions drawn in section 5.1.3. Initially, firms operate at the full-employment level of 100. Then, abruptly, the investment shock depresses output to 96. After that, output begins to recover, attaining a local maximum of 101.23. Later on, output passes through a local minimum of 100.01. The major difference, however, is that output now takes off forever. This outcome can be attributed to the fact that here the government must pay interest on public debt. Figure 2 graphs the corresponding time path of public debt. Public debt starts at zero, soars until 1.01, then plummets to 0.31 and finally proliferates without bounds.

Owing to the subsequent overemployment, money wages will spring up. This compels firms to mark up prices, thereby contracting real balances. As a

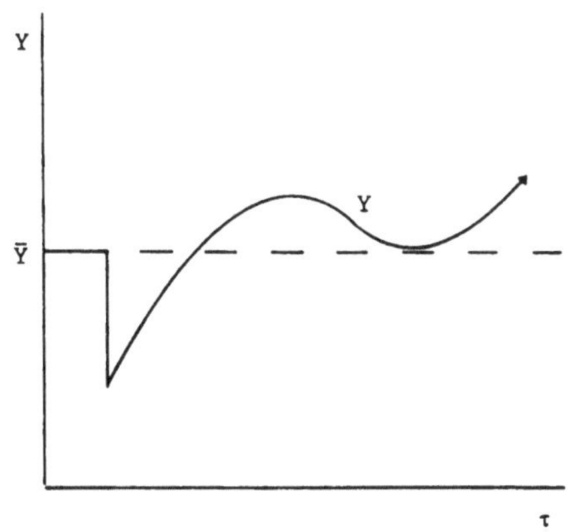

Figure 1. Output Cycle.

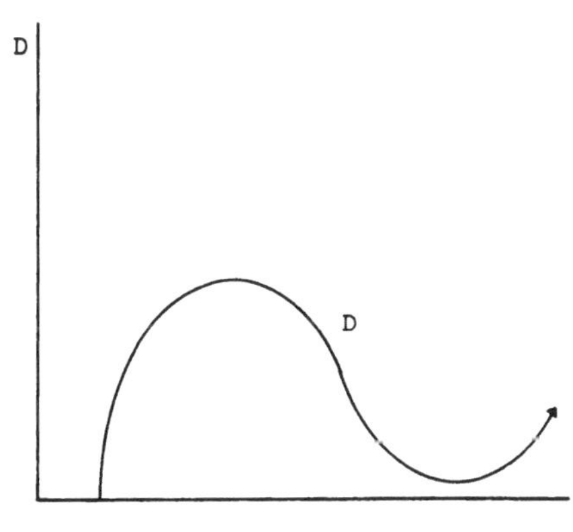

Figure 2. Public Debt Cycle.

consequence, the rate of interest goes up, which curbs private investment. More exactly, private investment becomes negative, thus the stock of capital declines. Ultimately, this process drives output down to zero, in full analogy to chapter 3 and section 4.4.

Essentially, the process of adjustment can be divided into three phases. Initially, the economy is in the long-run equilibrium. Above all, the labour market clears. Firms do not invest, so the stock of capital is uniform. The budget is balanced, and no public debt does exist. In the first phase, sales expectations worsen autonomously. Therefore, businesses postpone the replacement of capital. Net investment becomes negative, thus reducing the stock of capital. As a result, enterprises have to dismiss workers. The diminution in income entails a diminution in tax proceeds. The budget moves into a deficit, so public debt begins to grow.

In the second phase, sales expectations improve again. Firms make up for the replacement of capital. Now private investment becomes positive, replenishing the stock of capital. Accordingly, the economy switches from underemployment to overemployment. Besides, the increase in income causes an increase in tax earnings. The budget gets into a surplus, which involves that public debt is being retired. But in the long-run, public debt tends to explode. Eventually, this squeezes the stock of capital to zero, so there will be fatal crowding out.

In summary, the investment shock generates a cyclical process of adjustment. The budget, however, will not be balanced over the cycle. Put differently, the long-run equilibrium proves to be unstable. At long last, the economy will break down.

Finally, we shall confront these findings with the results obtained in chapter 5, where public interest had been neglected. On the one hand, the two economies agree in comparative statics. On the other hand, they differ sharply with respect to stability.

6.2. Economy With Fiscal Policy

In the current section, we shall postulate that the government adheres to an active fiscal policy. Strictly speaking, the government adapts public consumption so as to preserve full employment, while leaving the tax rate unaffected.

To begin with, in section 6.2.1., we shall remember the overlapping generations model. There, the presentation will center around the long-run equilibrium. Then, in section 6.2.2., we shall install the multiplier-accelerator model. In that place, the process of adjustment will be examined in greater detail. At the end, the two approaches will be tied together.

Table 17

Investment Shock and Passive Fiscal Policy

t	E	K*	K	I	D	iD	Y	G	T	B
0	100	100	100	0	0	0	100	20	20	0
1	90	90	100	- 2	0	0	96	20	19.2	0.8
2	96	96	98	- 0.4	0.8	0.08	99.28	20	19.87	0.21
3	99.28	99.28	97.6	0.34	1.01	0.10	100.78	20	20.18	- 0.08
4	100.78	100.78	97.94	0.57	0.93	0.09	101.23	20	20.26	- 0.17
5	101.23	101.23	98.51	0.54	0.76	0.08	101.16	20	20.25	- 0.17
6	101.16	101.16	99.05	0.42	0.59	0.06	100.90	20	20.19	- 0.13
7	100.90	100.90	99.47	0.29	0.46	0.05	100.63	20	20.14	- 0.09
8	100.63	100.63	99.76	0.17	0.37	0.04	100.38	20	20.08	- 0.04
9	100.38	100.38	99.93	0.09	0.33	0.03	100.21	20	20.05	- 0.02
10	100.21	100.21	100.01	0.04	0.31	0.03	100.11	20	20.03	0
11	100.11	100.11	100.05	0.01	0.31	0.03	100.05	20	20.02	0.01
12	100.05	100.05	100.06	0.00	0.32	0.03	100.03	20	20.01	0.02
13	100.03	100.03	100.06	- 0.01	0.34	0.03	100.01	20	20.01	0.02
14	100.01	100.01	100.05	- 0.01	0.36	0.04	100.02	20	20.01	0.03

6.2.1. Overlapping Generations Model

The long-run equilibrium can be described by a system of three equations, see (20) until (23) in section 3.1.:

(1) $$Y = K^{\alpha} N^{\beta}$$

(2) $$K = \beta\delta(1-t)Y$$

(3) $$G = tY$$

The budget is balanced. At the outset, let there be no public debt, so public consumption matches tax revenue. Here α, β, δ, G and N are given exogenously, whereas t, K and Y are endogenous variables. There are as many variables as unknowns, so the system is definite. The long-run equilibrium reveals the following properties, as is familiar. Labour supply, the stock of capital and output are invariant. Firms abstain from investment. Households and the government take in all of output.

Initially, the economy is in the long-run equilibrium. Then, suddenly, an investment shock happens. More precisely, sales expectations deteriorate. In due course, the economy gravitates to a new long-run equilibrium. In addition, the post-shock steady state coincides with the pre-shock steady state, since all parameters of the model are constant.

6.2.2. Multiplier-Accelerator Model

It is still convenient to abstract from the money market. At first, we shall establish the short-run equilibrium. Later on, we shall ascertain the long-run equilibrium.

Let us begin with the short-run equilibrium. We shall suppose that the government pursues an active fiscal policy. Strictly speaking, the government varies public consumption G so as to maintain full employment $Y = \bar{Y}$. Moreover, the government imposes a tax at the flat rate $t = \text{const.}$ on both factor income and debt income $T = t(\bar{Y} + iD)$. By definition, the budget deficit shows the excess of public consumption and public interest over tax revenue $B = G + iD - T$ or $B = G + iD - t(\bar{Y} + iD)$. Public borrowing period by period contributes to the accumulation of public debt $D_{+1} = D + B$.

Factor income and debt income, diminished by taxation, provide disposable income $Y_d = \bar{Y} + iD - T$. By resorting to the tax function, this can be written as $Y_d = (1-t)(\bar{Y} + iD)$. Besides, private consumption is a linear function of disposable income $C = \bar{C} + c(1-t)(\bar{Y} + iD)$. Here it is useful to return to the starting point. The government accommodates public consumption G in such a way that full employment always prevails $Y = \bar{Y}$, as has already been mentioned above. Output can be dedicated to private consumption, private investment and public consumption $\bar{Y} = C + I + G$. Now insert the consumption function and solve for the required volume of public consumption $G = \bar{G} - I - c(1-t)iD$, where $\bar{G}$ symbolizes the stationary level.

Further, private investment serves to fill the gap between the desired stock of capital and the actual stock of capital $I = \lambda(K^* - K)$. The desired stock of capital depends on sales expectations $K^* = vE$, where v denotes the capital-output ratio. Expected sales, in turn, generally move at the full employment level $E = \bar{Y}$. Apparently, private investment augments the stock of capital $K_{+1} = K + I$.

To sum up, the short-run equilibrium can be compressed into a system of nine equations:

(1) $$\bar{Y} = C + I + G$$
(2) $$C = \bar{C} + c(1-t)(\bar{Y} + iD)$$
(3) $$I = \lambda(K^* - K)$$
(4) $$K^* = vE$$
(5) $$E = \bar{Y}$$
(6) $$K_{+1} = K + I$$
(7) $$G = \bar{G} - I - c(1-t)iD$$
(8) $$B = G + iD - t(\bar{Y} + iD)$$
(9) $$D_{+1} = D + B$$

At this juncture, we leave the short-run equilibrium and turn to the long-run equilibrium. In the steady state, the stock of capital is uniform $K_{+1} = K$. Substitute this into (6) to arrive at:

(10) $$I = 0$$

That is to say, firms dispense with investment. Next eliminate I in (3) with the help of (10) to obtain $K^* = K$. Then put this together with (5) into (4) to get:

(11) $$K = v\bar{Y}$$

In the steady state, public debt does not change either $D_{+1} = D$. Now combine this with (9):

(12) $$B = 0$$

In other words, the budget is balanced. Finally, insert this together with $G = \bar{G}$ into (8) and rearrange:

(13) $$\bar{G} + iD = t(\bar{Y} + iD)$$

The technology is of the Leontief type:

$$Y = \min\left(\frac{K}{v}, \frac{\bar{N}}{a}\right) \tag{14}$$

Once again, if the resource constraint is binding, it will do so only in a soft way.

We assume that there is no public debt in the long-run equilibrium before disturbance. For $D=0$, (13) simplifies to $\bar{G}=t\,\bar{Y}$. Besides, we posit that the labour market clears in the long-run equilibrium before disturbance $\bar{Y}=\bar{N}/a$. Now substitute (2), (10) and $G=\bar{G}$ into (1), observing $D=0$ as well as $\bar{G}=t\,\bar{Y}$:

$$\bar{Y} = \frac{\bar{C}}{1-c} + \bar{G} \tag{15}$$

Let this condition be satisfied. Beyond that, solve $\bar{G}=t\,\bar{Y}$ for t, taking account of (15):

$$t = \frac{(1-c)\,\bar{G}}{\bar{C}+(1-c)\,\bar{G}} \tag{16}$$

Let this requirement also be met.

Initially, the economy is in the stationary equilibrium. Then, abruptly, sales expectations deteriorate. As a response, the government adjusts fiscal policy so as to avoid unemployment. As time proceeds, the economy converges to a new stationary equilibrium. What is more, the post-shock steady state is identical to the pre-shock steady state. Eventually, the stock of capital comes back to its original value. This can be ascribed to the fact that no parameter has been touched and that sales expectations adapt themselves appropriately.

How does public debt develop over the transition as a whole? As a baseline, take the budget constraint $\bar{G}+iD=t(\bar{Y}+iD)$. In the old steady state, public consumption was assumed to equal tax earnings $\bar{G}=t\,\bar{Y}$. In the new steady state, this is valid too, since $\bar{G}$, t and $\bar{Y}$ are fixed. Now put $\bar{G}=t\,\bar{Y}$ into the budget constraint to get $iD=0$ and $D=0$. At the end, as a result, public debt will entirely be paid off.

Last but not least, the overlapping generations model will be coupled with the multiplier-accelerator model. We postulate that the two models agree in the long-run equilibrium before disturbance. Then, as a consequence, they agree in the long-run equilibrium after disturbance as well. In this way, the two approaches amalgamate.

6.2.3. Simulation

In the current section, we shall compute the process of adjustment set in motion by an investment shock. Table 18 presents an overview of the trajectory under active fiscal policy. The calculations rest again on the following parameter values: $c = 0.625$, $t = 0.2$, $\bar{C} = 30$, $\bar{G} = 20$, $v = 1$, $\lambda = 0.2$, $a = 1$, $\bar{N} = 100$ and $i = 0.1$.

At the beginning, in period 0, the economy moves in the steady state. Firms manufacture a homogeneous commodity $Y = 100$ by means of capital $K = 100$ and labour $N = 100$. Particularly, all workers find a job. Private and public consumption add up to income $C + G = 100$. Businesses refrain from investment $I = 0$. At the start, let there be no public debt $D = 0$. The budget is balanced $B = 0$, so tax revenue matches public consumption $T = G$.

Against this background, in period 1, an investment shock occurs. More precisely, expected sales drop from 100 to 90. Owing to that, enterprises reduce the desired stock of capital from 100 to 90. The actual stock of capital, on the other hand, has been inherited from the past, hence it cannot change. Therefore, private investment is cut back from 0 to -2. Still no public debt does exist, as the budget was balanced in period 0. For the moment, the government has to pay no interest.

In order to close the ensuing gap in aggregate demand, the government increases public consumption from 20 to 22, according to $G = \bar{G} - I - c(1-t)iD$. Output stays at 100, thus the labour market continues to clear. Tax proceeds do not vary $T = t(\bar{Y} + iD) = 20$, because public interest still amounts to zero. As a consequence, the fiscal expansion brings the budget into a deficit of 2, confer $B = G + iD - t(\bar{Y} + iD)$.

Then, in period 2, expected sales return to 100, since actual sales have not been impaired. Analogously, businesses correct the desired stock of capital upwards from 90 to 100. The actual stock of capital, by way of contrast, declines from 100 to 98, due to the negative investment carried out in period 1. By virtue of the accelerator, private investment jumps up from -2 to $+0.4$. Further, the budget deficit incurred in period 1 gives rise to a public debt of 2. Likewise, public interest goes up from 0 to 0.2.

In order to absorb the resulting excess in aggregate demand, fiscal policy switches over from expansion to contraction. Strictly speaking, the government lowers public consumption from 22 to 19.5. Output remains unaffected, so enterprises still engage all workers. Besides, tax earnings come up slightly from 20 to 20.04, even though factor income does not move. Over and above that, the budget deficit of 2 turns into a surplus of 0.34. This process reiterates itself round by round.

Next we shall deal with the long-run effects. Public consumption obeys the law $G = \bar{G} - I - c(1-t)iD$, where I approaches zero. For the numerical example, this equation can be stated as $G = 20 - 0.5\,iD$. Substitute this into the budget constraint $B = G + iD - t(\bar{Y} + iD)$ to arrive at $B = 0.3\,iD$. That means, the given budget deficit elevates public debt. The accompanying increase in public interest aggravates the budget deficit, what speeds up the growth of public debt, and so on. In other words, public debt tends to explode. Conversely, on account of $G = 20 - 0.5\,iD$, public consumption tends to implode.

Naturally, however, public consumption cannot fall below zero. As soon as this point is reached, the government can no longer prevent overemployment from coming into existence. Accordingly, money wages and prices start to climb, thereby reducing real balances. The rise in the rate of interest restrains private investment, so the stock of capital dwindles away. Ultimately, in full analogy to the third chapter and to section 4.4., the stock of capital shrinks back to zero.

By and large, the process of adjustment can be split up into three phases. Initially, the economy is in the stationary equilibrium. Especially, all workers find a job. Firms abstain from investment, so the stock of capital does not vary. The budget is balanced, and no public debt does exist. In the first phase, sales expectations worsen. Private investment becomes negative, hence the stock of capital begins to decline. In order to fight unemployment, the government lifts public consumption. The budget gets into a deficit, so public debt accumulates.

In the second phase, sales expectations recover. Private investment turns positive, thereby replenishing the stock of capital. In order to combat overemployment, the government curtails public consumption. The budget moves into a surplus, thus redeeming public debt. But in the third phase, public debt is liable to explode, which brings the stock of capital down to zero. Eventually, there will be fatal crowding out.

In summary, the investment shock induces a cyclical process of adjustment. This, in turn, calls for a cyclical path of fiscal policy. In spite of this, the budget will not be balanced across the cycle. What is more, the long-run equilibrium proves to be unstable. That is to say, finally the economy will collapse.

Last but not least, the results obtained here will be confronted with the conclusions drawn for an economy without public interest, confer section 5.3.3. There, the steady state was shown to be stable. On the one hand, the two models agree in comparative statics. On the other hand, they differ dramatically in the long-run dynamics.

6.2.4. Restoring Stability

Fiscal policy safeguards full employment against investment shocks. In the long run, however, it drives output down to zero, so the economy will break down. How can the government escape this dilemma? In the current section, we shall explore two distinct strategies. First: Tax finance of public interest at full employment. And second: The government pays off the residual of public debt at full employment.

Let us begin with tax finance of public interest at full employment. For an economy without public interest, the long-run equilibrium is stable. Yet for an economy with public interest, the steady state is unstable. In this situation, it is the task of government to restore stability. As a first means to accomplish this end, we shall discuss tax finance of public interest. Obviously, public interest can be viewed as a transfer payment. Under tax finance, the transfer multiplier amounts to zero, as is well known. Therefore, tax finance of public interest allows to neutralize the demand-side effects of public interest.

Tax finance of public interest involves:

$$t(\bar{Y}+iD)=\bar{G}+iD \tag{1}$$

Properly speaking, tax revenue serves to cover the steady-state level of public consumption plus the interest payments on public debt. At the same time, the government manages aggregate demand to warrant full employment:

$$\bar{Y}=\frac{\bar{C}+I+G+c(1-t)iD}{1-c(1-t)} \tag{2}$$

This system can be solved recursively. In the first step, the government sets the tax rate according to equation (1). Then, given the tax rate, the government selects public consumption as prescribed by equation (2).

In principle, the government tries to reach two goals, full employment and long-run stability. In doing this, the government has two instruments at its disposal, public consumption and the tax rate. In the following way, the two means should be allocated to the two ends: The government should vary public consumption so as to keep up full employment, while it should adjust the tax rate so as to maintain stability.

To illustrate this, consider the numerical simulation conducted in the preceding section. The key question is: What difference does tax finance of public interest make? For periods 0 and 1, evidently, the two economies coincide, see table 18.

Now period 2 will be looked into in greater detail. Both expected sales and the desired stock of capital equal 100. The actual stock of capital has been determined in the past as 98. Corresponding to the speed of adjustment, private investment takes on the value 0.4. The government pays the interest rate 0.1 on public debt 2, so public interest amounts to 0.2. By virtue of equation (1), the required tax rate is 0.2016. Then put this into equation (2) and solve for the necessary volume of public consumption 19.60. As a consequence, output stays at 100, hence the labour market still clears. Finally, evaluate the budget constraint $B=G+iD-t(\bar{Y}+iD)$ to arrive at a surplus of 0.4. Apparently, this agrees with the results obtained for the economy without public interest, compare section 5.3.3.

In general terms, the time path with tax finance of public interest is identical to the time path without public interest, confer table 10. The only exception to this rule is given by the tax rate. Under tax finance of public interest, as a fundamental result, a long-run equilibrium does in fact exist. What is more, the long-run equilibrium proves to be stable, as has been demonstrated above. This underlines the importance of the conclusions drawn in section 5.3.3.

At this point, we leave the tax finance of public interest and turn to the amortization of public debt. Imagine that the government pays off the rest of public debt at full employment:

$$t(\bar{Y} + iD) = G + iD + D \tag{3}$$

That is to say, tax receipts serve to cover the sum of public consumption, public interest and public debt. In addition, the government controls aggregate demand in such a way that underemployment as well as overemployment are circumvented, compare equation (2). From equations (2) and (3), similarly, one can deduce the tax rate and public consumption.

To see this more clearly, regard table 18 in the previous section. There, public debt reaches a local minimum in period 15. For that reason, period 15 seems to be the best date to retire public debt. Both expected sales and the desired stock of capital move at the steady-state level of 100. The actual stock of capital comes close to 100, thus private investment is very small 0.02. The government pays the interest rate 0.1 on public debt 0.51, hence public interest amounts to 0.05.

Now insert these values into (3) to get $G = 100.05\,t - 0.56$. Then eliminate G in (2). This provides the tax rate needed to do the job $t = 0.2135$. Finally substitute the tax rate into $G = 100.05\,t - 0.56$, which yields public consumption $G = 20.80$. Under these circumstances, output remains unaffected at 100, so full employment still prevails. The budget surplus of 0.51 equals the residual of public debt being redeemed.

At this stage, we close period 15 and open up period 16. Both expected sales and the desired stock of capital are uniform 100, whereas the actual stock of capital is 99.91. Private investment amounts to 0.02. Public debt does no longer exist, therefore the government needs not to pay interest any more. In order to secure full employment, the government adapts public consumption to 19.95. And to balance the budget, the government sets the tax rate at 0.1995. This process repeats itself round by round. The multiplier-accelerator model without public debt is stable, as has been mentioned before.

Accordingly, figure 1 plots the time path of public debt. Without loss of generality, we posit that at the start there is no public debt. In the first phase, the investment shock brings the budget into a deficit, thereby building up public debt. In the second phase, the budget exhibits a surplus, thus public debt is being amortized. In the third phase, however, public debt tends to explode. In other

Table 18

Investment Shock and Active Fiscal Policy

τ	E	K*	K	I	D	iD	G	Y	T	B
0	100	100	100	0	0	0	20	100	20	0
1	90	90	100	- 2	0	0	22	100	20	2
2	100	100	98	0.4	2	0.2	19.5	100	20.04	- 0.34
3	100	100	98.4	0.32	1.66	0.17	19.60	100	20.03	- 0.26
4	100	100	98.72	0.26	1.40	0.14	19.67	100	20.03	- 0.22
5	100	100	98.98	0.20	1.18	0.12	19.74	100	20.02	- 0.16
6	100	100	99.18	0.16	1.02	0.10	19.79	100	20.02	- 0.13
7	100	100	99.34	0.13	0.89	0.09	19.83	100	20.02	- 0.10
8	100	100	99.47	0.11	0.79	0.08	19.85	100	20.02	- 0.09
9	100	100	99.58	0.08	0.70	0.07	19.89	100	20.01	- 0.05
10	100	100	99.64	0.07	0.65	0.07	19.90	100	20.01	- 0.04
11	100	100	99.71	0.06	0.61	0.06	19.91	100	20.01	- 0.04
12	100	100	99.77	0.05	0.57	0.06	19.92	100	20.01	- 0.03
13	100	100	99.82	0.04	0.54	0.05	19.94	100	20.01	- 0.02
14	100	100	99.86	0.03	0.52	0.05	19.95	100	20.01	- 0.01
15	100	100	99.89	0.02	0.51	0.05	19.96	100	20.01	0
16	100	100	99.91	0.02	0.51	0.05	19.96	100	20.01	0
17	100	100	99.93	0.01	0.51	0.05	19.97	100	20.01	0.01
18	100	100	99.94	0.01	0.52	0.05	19.97	100	20.01	0.01
19	100	100	99.95	0.01	0.53	0.05	19.97	100	20.01	0.01

words, public debt attains a local minimum at time τ^*. This appears to be the best opportunity to retire public debt altogether.

To summarize, the investment shock generates a cyclical process of adjustment. This in turn calls for a cyclical path of fiscal policy. Here the government pursues two objectives. On the one hand, it seeks to maintain full employment. On the other hand, it wishes to keep up long-run stability. In doing this, the government maximizes consumption (per head). There are many time paths of fiscal policy which achieve this, as can easily be seen. So the government may choose among them in a pragmatic manner. In any case, a necessary condition is that the budget must be balanced over the cycle.

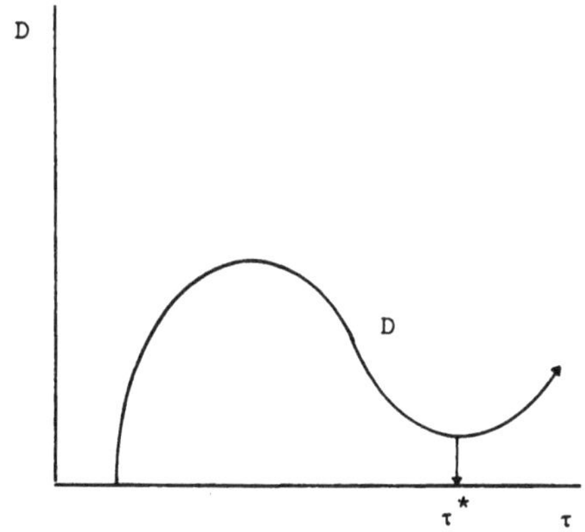

Figure 1. Cyclical Budget Balance.

Appendix

Another solution consists in balancing the budget each period. More exactly, the government fixes the tax rate. In addition, the government accommodates public consumption to tax proceeds. That is, during a recession the government lowers public consumption. Conversely, during a boom the government raises public consumption. On that account, the budget will be balanced each period, hence no public debt does exist. Over and above that, the long-run equilibrium will be stable, confer the economy without public sector studied in section 5.1. As as result, the transitory shock will have no permanent consequences.

Against this background, Buchanan (1977) pleads for continuous budget balance. On the one hand, to be fair, this fiscal policy will prevent the secular breakdown. On the other hand, it will amplify the cyclical movements. In the case of a recession, the tight fiscal policy will make unemployment even worse. My personal opinion is that, after all, this seems not to be the best strategy, to say the least.

So far, the analysis was confined to adverse shocks. Of course, it must be admitted that favourable shocks can occur, too. Therefore, one may argue that the negative and positive disturbances will tend to cancel each other. Strictly speaking, a contractionary investment shock leaves a residual of public debt, as has been shown above. By the same token, an expansionary investment shock, due to improved sales expectations, leaves a remainder of public wealth. Now the residual of public debt and the remainder of public wealth are liable to cross out one another, thus helping to avoid the final collapse.

6.3. Stability

In the current section, we shall investigate a rather simple economy with public debt. Here the accent will be put on dynamics and stability.

Firms produce as much as households, firms and the government want to buy $Y = C + I + G$. Private consumption is a linear function of disposable income $C = \bar{C} + c Y_d$. Factor income and debt income, net after tax respectively, constitute disposable income $Y_d = Y + iD - T$. The rate of interest is supposed to be fixed $i = \text{const}$. Private investment as well as public consumption are given exogenously $I = \bar{I}$ and $G = \bar{G}$. The government levies a proportional tax on both factor income and debt income $T = t(Y + iD)$. As usual, the budget deficit is defined as the excess of public consumption and public interest over tax revenue $B = G + iD - T$. What is more, public borrowing adds to public debt $D_{+1} = D + B$. Next insert the tax function into $Y_d = Y + iD - T$ and regroup $Y_d = (1-t)(Y + iD)$. Then eliminate Y_d in the consumption function to reach $C = \bar{C} + c(1-t)(Y + iD)$. Likewise, substitute the tax function into the budget constraint $B = \bar{G} + iD - t(Y + iD)$.

Accordingly, the short-run equilibrium can be described by a system of three equations:

(1) $$Y = \bar{C} + c(1-t)(Y + iD) + \bar{I} + \bar{G}$$

(2) $$B = \bar{G} + iD - t(Y + iD)$$

(3) $$D_{+1} = D + B$$

We come now to the long-run equilibrium. In the steady state, public debt does not move $D_{+1} = D$. Put this into (3) to get:

(4) $$B = 0$$

In other words, the budget will be balanced. Therefore, the long-run equilibrium can be condensed into a system of two equations:

(5) $$Y = \bar{C} + c(1-t)(Y + iD) + \bar{I} + \bar{G}$$

(6) $$\bar{G} + iD = t(Y + iD)$$

Here, c, i, t, $\bar{C}$, $\bar{G}$ and $\bar{I}$ are given exogenously, while D and Y are endogenous variables. The number of equations matches the number of unknowns, so the system is definite.

In the next step, we shall derive the stationary level of the endogenous variables. First of all, solve (6) for D:

$$D = \frac{tY - \bar{G}}{i(1-t)} \tag{7}$$

Then combine this with (5) to infer the steady-state value of output:

$$Y = \frac{\bar{C} + \bar{I}}{1-c} + \bar{G} \tag{8}$$

It is remarkable, that neither the interest rate nor the tax rate have any influence on the stationary level. Besides, from (8) one can deduce both the private investment multiplier and the government purchase multiplier:

$$\Delta Y = \frac{1}{1-c} \Delta \bar{I} \tag{9}$$

$$\Delta Y = \Delta \bar{G} \tag{10}$$

Here the question arises, how the long-run multiplier compares with the short-run multiplier. Let us begin with the private investment multiplier. In the short run, it amounts to:

$$\Delta Y = \frac{1}{1-c(1-t)} \Delta \bar{I} \tag{11}$$

as is familiar. As a consequence, the long-run multiplier exceeds the short-run multiplier. We turn now to the government purchase multiplier, which in the short run also equals:

$$\Delta Y = \frac{1}{1-c(1-t)} \Delta \bar{G} \tag{12}$$

Owing to that, the long-run multiplier falls short of the short-run multiplier, as opposed to the case considered before. The last point refers to the tax multiplier. In the short-run, an increase in the tax rate leads to a reduction in output. Thus the long-run multiplier is smaller than the short-run multiplier, speaking in absolute terms.

Analogously, figures 1, 2 and 3 visualize the comparative statics of output. To start with, figure 1 depicts the time path engendered by a favourable investment shock. In the short-run, the disturbance raises output. And in the long-run, it enhances output even more. Correspondingly, figure 2 displays how output evolves due to a fiscal expansion. In the short period, the loose fiscal policy lifts output substantially. In the long period, however, output settles down at an intermediate level. Finally, figure 3 graphs the trajectory of output under a tax increase. In the short term, the adverse shock depresses output. But in the long term, output regains its initial position.

Last but not least, what is the long-run impact on public debt? To answer this question, insert (8) into (7) and reshuffle adequately:

$$D = \frac{t(\bar{C} + \bar{I})}{i(1-c)(1-t)} - \frac{\bar{G}}{i} \tag{13}$$

As a result, an increase in public consumption brings about a decline in public debt. And a tax rise causes a rise in public debt. At a glance, both findings seem to be like a paradox.

At this juncture, we close the comparative statics and open up the dynamics. Here we shall concentrate on the problem of stability. It is convenient to express the budget constraint (2) as $B = \bar{G} + R - t(Y + R)$, where $R = iD$ denotes public interest. First take differences and collect terms $\Delta B = (1-t)\Delta R - t\Delta Y$. Now what we are interested in is the condition for the change in public borrowing to be negative:

$$\frac{1-t}{t} < \frac{\Delta Y}{\Delta R} \tag{14}$$

Then take differences of the goods market equation (1) to obtain:

$$\frac{\Delta Y}{\Delta R} = \frac{c(1-t)}{1-c(1-t)} \tag{15}$$

Finally eliminate $\Delta Y / \Delta R$ in (14) by means of (15) to arrive at $c > 1$. That means, if the marginal propensity to consume is above unity, the increment in the budget deficit will decline. Conversely, if the marginal propensity is below unity, the increment in the budget deficit will grow. In the real world, the condition $c > 1$ will be violated. On that account, public debt will tend to explode. What is more, this applies independently of the interest rate.

To sum up, a long-run equilibrium does indeed exist. Unfortunately, however, it proves to be unstable. What is more, this holds true for permanent shocks as well as for transitory shocks. Here again public debt acts like a virus which breeds itself. On the other hand, the government may well stabilize the economy by adapting public consumption and the tax rate appropriately.

Accordingly, figures 4, 5, 6 and 7 illustrate the dynamics of output. To begin with, figure 4 plots the time path of output due to a fiscal expansion. At first, the increase in government purchases elevates output. Later on, output continues to climb without bounds. Conversely, figure 5 shows how output develops under a fiscal contraction. Initially, the reduction in government purchases depresses output. As time goes on, output keeps on falling until it hits the floor.

Figure 6 indicates the consequences of an "adverse" investment shock. Obviously, the trajectory can be divided into two phases. In the short-run, the disturbance lowers output. The cut in private investment curbs income and tax receipts, so the budget gets into a deficit. But in the long run, the government has to pay interest on public debt, thereby stimulating private consumption and output. This outcome is in marked contrast to the conclusions drawn just before.

The other way round, figure 7 reveals the impact of a "favourable" investment shock. Once again, the process of transmission can be split up into two phases. In the short-run, the disruption raises output. Yet in the long-run, the government receives interest on public assets, thus restraining private consumption and output.

At last, we shall simulate the process of adjustment kicked off by a loose fiscal policy. Table 19 permits to follow the time path step by step. The numerical example will be based on the subsequent parameter values: $c = 0.625$, $t = 0.2$, $\bar{C} = 20$, $\bar{I} = 10$, $\bar{G} = 20$ and $i = 0.1$. In the long-run equilibrium, output amounts to 100, as can easily be seen from equation (8). Correspondingly, equation (13) yields that public debt vanishes in this situation.

Originally, in period 0, the economy reproduces itself in the steady state. The government buys 20 units of goods and services. At the outset, no public debt does exist. Likewise, the government has to pay no interest. Aggregate demand equals 100, hence firms manufacture 100 units. The government takes in 20 units of taxes, so the budget is balanced.

Under these circumstances, in period 1, the government increases public consumption from 20 to 40. Public debt does not respond immediately, since it has been decided on in period 0. The same is valid for public interest. By virtue of

$$Y = \frac{\bar{C} + c(1-t)iD + \bar{I} + \bar{G}}{1 - c(1-t)} \tag{16}$$

the fiscal expansion lifts aggregate demand from 100 to 140. For that reason, businesses enhance output from 100 to 140, too. On account of $T = t\,(Y + i\,D)$, the rise in income is associated with a rise in tax earnings from 20 to 28. Owing to the budget constraint (2), the government must borrow 12 units.

At this stage, we leave period 1 and enter period 2. Henceforth, government purchases stay at the new level of 40. Public debt springs up from 0 to 12, due to the budget deficit incurred in period 1. Therefore, the government must pay 1.2 units of public interest. This, in turn, propels aggregate demand from 140 to 141.2. To the same degree, enterprises push up output. Tax proceeds improve from 28 to 28.5. Nevertheless, the budget deficit grows from 12 to 12.7. By comparison, the steady state level of output amounts to 120, confer equation (8). As a consequence, output is inclined to blow up.

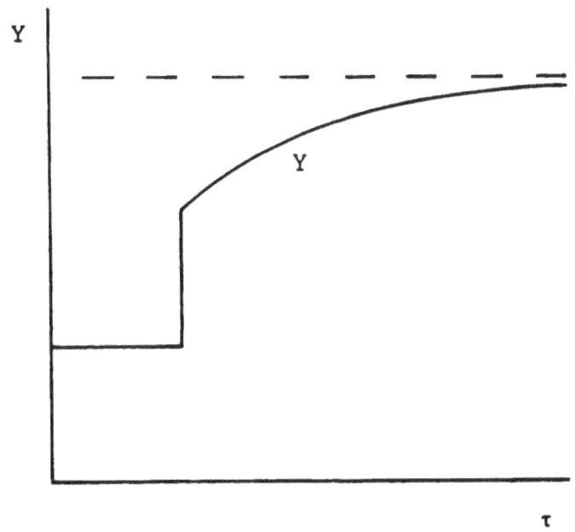

Figure 1. Increase in Private Investment (Comparative Statics).

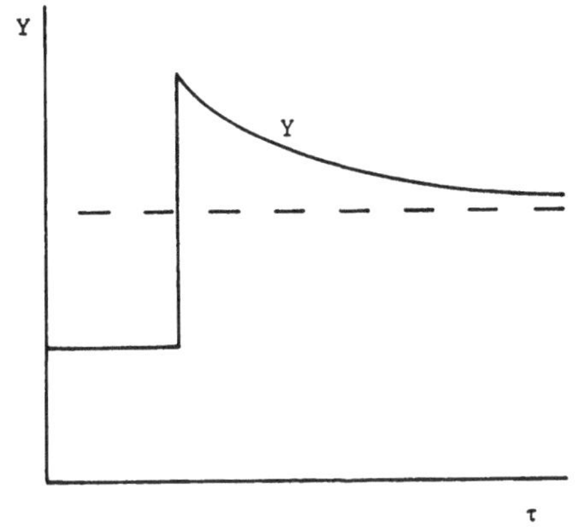

Figure 2. Increase in Government Purchases (Comparative Statics).

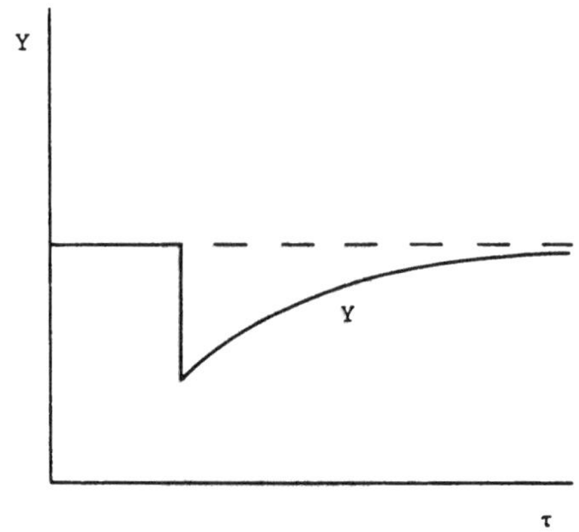

Figure 3. Tax Increase (Comparative Statics).

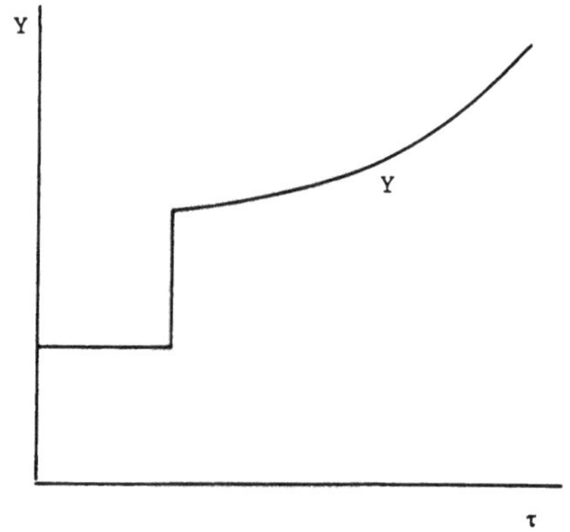

Figure 4. Increase in Government Purchases (Dynamics).

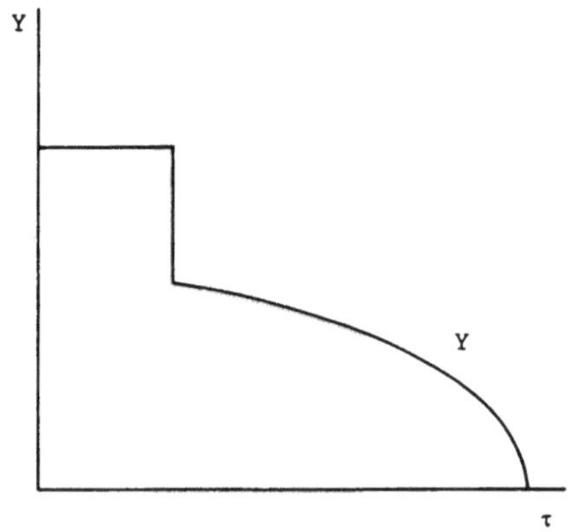

Figure 5. Reduction in Government Purchases (Dynamics).

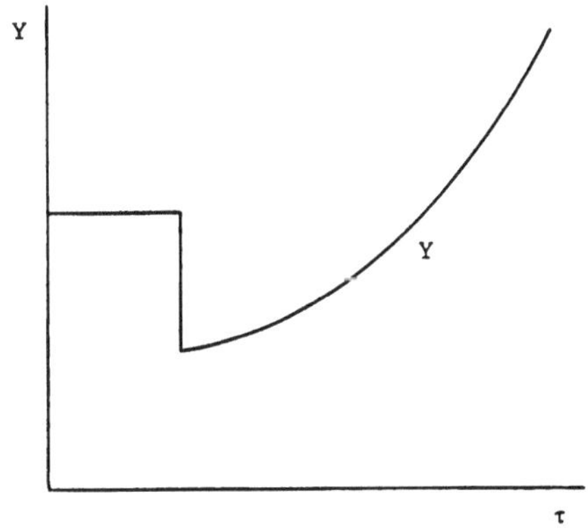

Figure 6. Reduction in Private Investment (Dynamics).

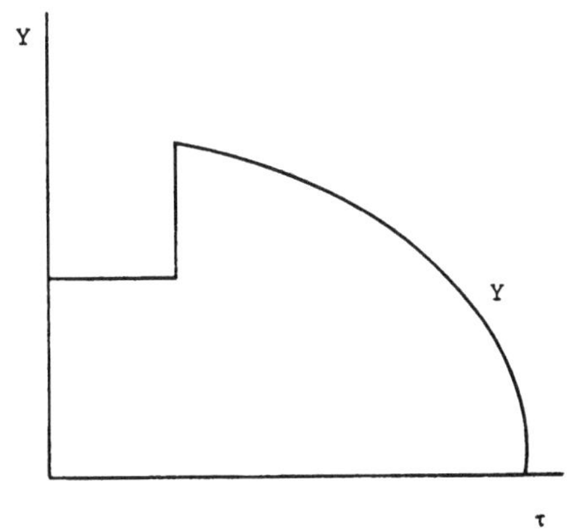

Figure 7. Increase in Private Investment (Dynamics).

Table 19

Increase in Government Purchases and Process of Adjustment

τ	G	D	iD	Y	T	B
0	20	0	0	100	20	0
1	40	0	0	140	28	12
2	40	12	1.2	141.2	28.5	12.7
3	40	24.7	2.5	142.5	29.0	13.5
4	40	38.2	3.8	143.8	29.5	14.3
5	40	52.5	5.3	145.3	30.1	15.2

7. Extensions

In the current chapter, the analysis will be extended to include some more aspects. To begin with, in section 7.1., we shall take a closer look at the concept of full employment.Then, in section 7.2., emphasis will be laid on competing instruments to absorb an investment shock. Next, in section 7.3., we shall leave the investment shock and turn to a monetary disturbance. Finally, in section 7.4., a growing economy will be addressed instead of a stationary economy.

7.1. The Concept of Full Employment

The primary goal of fiscal policy is to restore full employment. How should this notion be stated within the framework of a cyclical model? Does full employment prevail at the ceiling of the process or at its average? Whether the budget can be balanced over the cycle or not crucially depends on the answer to this question.

In a stylized way, figure 1 shows the time path of output as it can be observed. Against this background, how should full employment be defined? Here, evidently, two alternatives offer themselves. First, full employment exists at the ceiling of the process. And second, full employment is given at the average of the process.

This issue is intimately connected with the objective of fiscal policy. What level of output does the government wish to maintain, 1 or 2? In the first case, the budget will always be in deficit. Therefore, public debt will tend to explode. Ultimately, the economy will break down, as has been demonstrated above. In the second case, however, the government may well balance the budget across the cycle, thus no problem will be involved.

Figures 2 and 3 present the business cycle in the IS-LM diagram. In figure 2, output fluctuates below full employment. In this situation, a cyclical budget balance is not feasible in the long run. Eventually, private capital will completely be crowded out by public debt. In figure 3, by way of contrast, output fluctuates around full employment. In this situation, a cyclical budget balance can indeed be sustained.

As a result, the government should try to stabilize output at the average of the business cycle. During the slump, the government should run a fiscal expansion, thereby accumulating public debt. During the boom, the government should switch over to a fiscal contraction, thus retiring public debt. In full analogy, the unemployment rate moves up and down around zero. Accordingly, it is the task of fiscal policy to reduce these fluctuations.

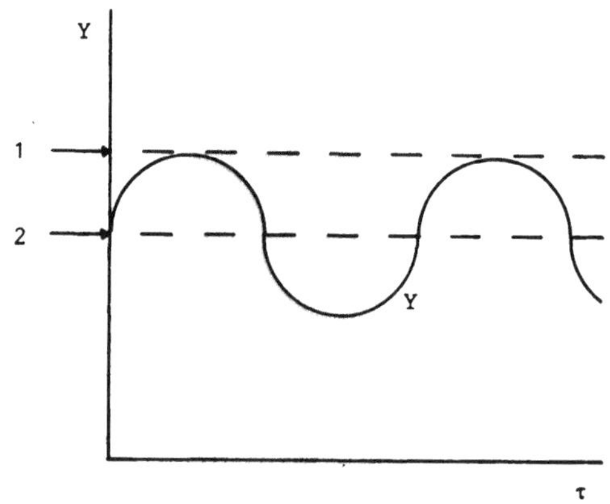

Figure 1. Targets of Fiscal Policy.

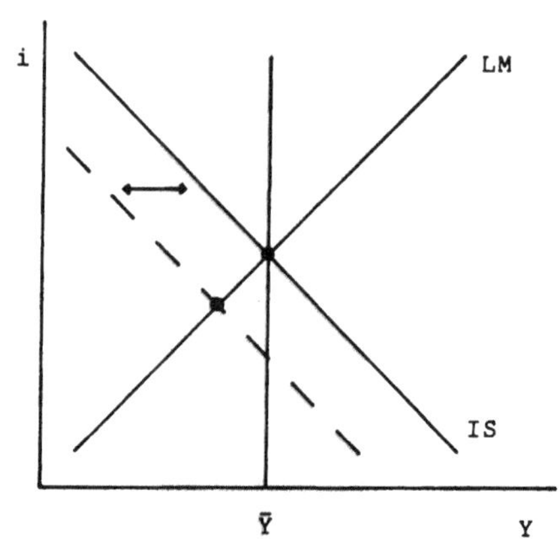

Figure 2. Business Cycle Below Full Employment.

Last but not least, we shall take account of structural unemployment, which can be attributed to both labour market frictions and structural change. In a stylized way, figure 4 visualizes the time path of unemployment. Strictly speaking, the rate of unemployment oscillates around the natural rate. When the actual rate u exceeds the natural rate $\bar{u}$, the government should adhere to a loose fiscal policy. Conversely, when the actual rate falls short of the natural rate, the government has to pursue a tight fiscal policy.

Political economy suggests that it is easy to lower unemployment during depression, while it is much more difficult to raise unemployment during prosperity, which jeopardizes cyclical budget balance. The only safe way out of this dilemma seems to be to ban public debt by constitution. Here the natural rate of unemployment can either be defined as the average of the actual rate or as the non-accelerating-inflation rate of unemployment, which makes no big difference. Now imagine that the government, instead, aims at the minimum level of unemployment. As luck would have it, this calls forth inflation and thwarts cyclical budget balance. Eventually, the economy will collapse.

In terms of the model, let $\bar{N}$ denote nominal labour supply and let F stand for labour market friction, so $\bar{N}-F$ symbolizes effective labour supply. Then full employment is characterized by the absence of structural unemployment $N=\bar{N}-F$. Correspondingly, full-employment output can be expressed as $\bar{Y}_N=(\bar{N}-F)/a$, whereas capacity output can still be written as $\bar{Y}_K=K/v$. In the long-run equilibrium, capacity output harmonizes with full-employment output $\bar{Y}=\bar{Y}_K=\bar{Y}_N$.

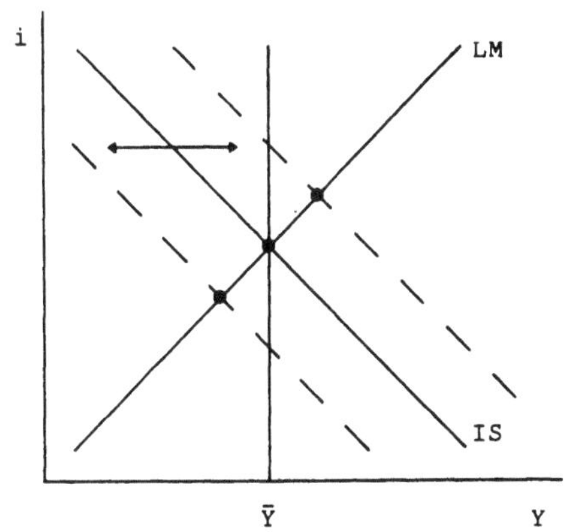

Figure 3. Business Cycle Around Full Employment.

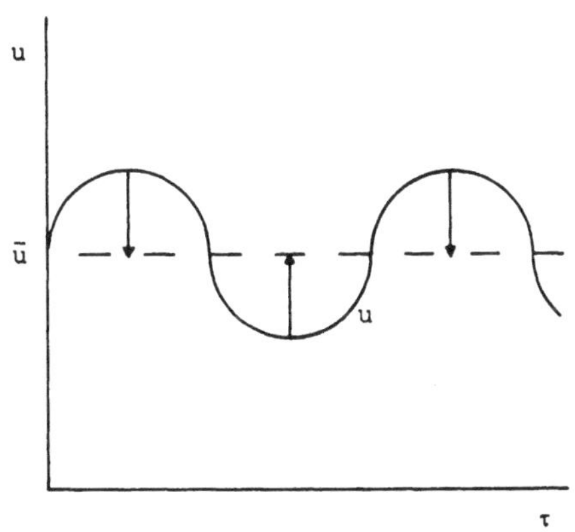

Figure 4. Business Cycle Around the Natural Rate of Unemployment.

7.2. Investment Shock

In the current section, we shall study alternative means of stabilization policy to overcome an investment shock. First, in section 7.2.1., money finance of the budget deficit will be investigated. After that, in section 7.2.2., we shall explore investment subsidies. At last, in section 7.2.3., monetary policy will enter the scene.

7.2.1. Money Finance of Budget Deficit

In the current section, money finance of the budget deficit will be sketched out briefly. To begin with, we shall consider an economy with public sector. Then, in a second step, we shall regard an economy where the government runs an active fiscal policy.

Let us start with an economy inclusive of a public sector. Again, the short-run equilibrium can be represented by a system of nine equations, confer (1) until (9) in section 5.2.2. The only difference is that here

(1) $$M_{+1} = M + B$$

is substituted for (9) $D_{+1} = D + B$. That is to say, the budget deficit is covered by money finance instead of by debt finance. As a consequence, the budget deficit adds to the quantity of money. Within this context, the demand-side effects of money finance are ignored. Yet this topic will be resumed later on.

Next we shall be concerned with the long-run equilibrium. The stock of capital does no longer change, so firms abstain from investment. Analogously, the quantity of money does no more vary, thus the budget is balanced. By virtue of the budget constraint, public consumption matches tax revenue. As a finding, expected sales leave no impact on the stationary level of output $Y = \bar{C}/(1-c) + \bar{G}$. Apparently, the reasoning closely follows the line taken in section 5.2.2.

Now suppose that, initially, the economy moves in the steady state. Then, abruptly, sales expectations worsen, thereby giving rise to an investment shock. Over time, the economy gravitates towards a new steady state. What is more, the post-shock steady state agrees with the pre-shock steady state. In other words, output, the stock of capital and labour demand return to their original position. In the final equilibrium, the labour market will clear again.This can be traced back to the postulate that all parameters are constant and that sales expectations adapt themselves.

How does the quantity of money behave over the process of adjustment as a whole? In answering this question, take differences of the budget constraint $B = \bar{G} - tY$ to arrive at $\Delta B = -t\Delta Y$. Then sum over all periods of the process $\Sigma\Delta B = -t\Sigma\Delta Y$, noting $\Sigma\Delta Y = 0$. As a result, one obtains $\Sigma\Delta B = 0$. That means, the terminal value of M coincides with the initial value of M. Therefore, money finance of the budget deficit exerts no lasting influence.

Here the simulation is identical to the experiment conducted for an economy with public sector but without public interest, see section 5.2.3. Hence the long-run equilibrium proves to be stable.

Figure 1 illustrates the time path, taking into account the demand-side effects of money finance. At the beginning, the economy is in the stationary equilibrium. Then, suddenly, sales expectations deteriorate. In the diagram, the IS curve shifts to the left. The budget gets into a deficit, so the quantity of money increases round by round. Accordingly, the LM curve goes slightly to the right. In the second phase, sales expectations recover, which pushes the IS curve substantially to the right. Now the budget exhibits a surplus, hence the quantity of money declines step by step. Correspondingly, the LM curve travels somewhat to the left. At the end, the economy comes back to its starting point.

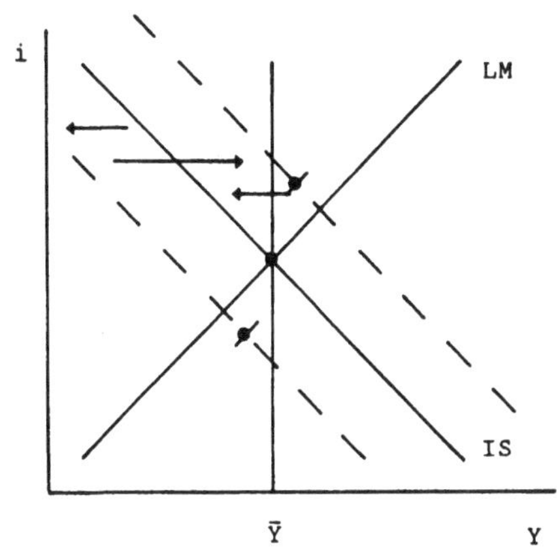

Figure 1. Investment Shock and Money Finance of Passive Fiscal Policy.

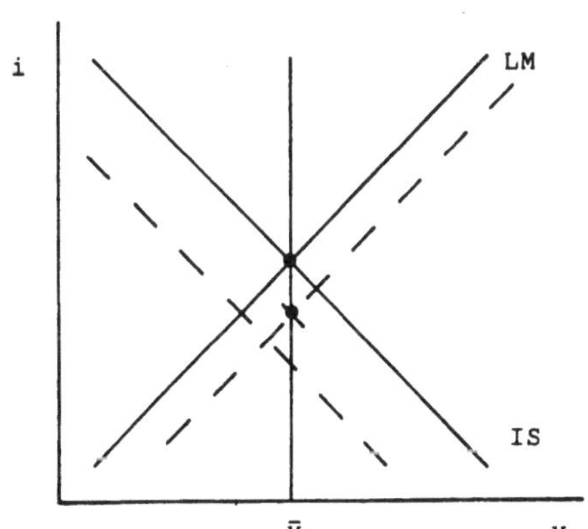

Figure 2. Investment Shock and Money Finance of Active Fiscal Policy.

In summary, the demand-side effects of money finance damp the cyclical reaction. Once more, this brings up the issue, whether the stationary equilibrium will turn out to be stable or not. Whatever the exact solution may be, the government is able to render the economy stable.

So far the government adhered to a passive fiscal policy. Now we shall posit that the government, instead, pursues an active fiscal policy. In the short-run equilibrium, $M_{+1} = M + B$ takes the place of equation (9) in section 5.3.2. For the moment, the demand-side effects of money finance will be neglected, see below.

Imagine that, initially, the economy is in the long-run equilibrium. Then, spontaneously, sales expectations worsen. In order to prevent unemployment from coming into existence, the government switches over to a fiscal expansion. As time goes on, the economy converges to a new long-run equilibrium. What is more, the post-shock steady state coincides with the pre-shock steady state.

Here the problem emerges how the quantity of money is affected by the process of adjustment. As a baseline, regard the budget constraint $B = G - tY$. Then take differences $\Delta B = \Delta G - t\Delta Y$, paying attention to $\Delta Y = 0$. Finally, sum over all periods of the process $\Sigma\Delta B = \Sigma\Delta G$ and observe $\Sigma\Delta G = 0$ to reach $\Sigma\Delta B = 0$. As a consequence, again, the terminal value of the quantity of money is identical to its original value.

The corresponding simulation completely agrees with the calculations performed for the economy with fiscal policy but without public interest, compare section 5.3.3. In full analogy, the long-run equilibrium proves to be stable.

Figure 2 graphs how the economy develops over time, incorporating the demand-side effects of money finance. At the beginning, the economy is in the stationary equilibrium. Then an investment shock happens, which shifts the IS schedule to the left. As a response, the government runs a loose fiscal policy, thereby moving the IS schedule back to the right. The budget gets into deficit, so the quantity of money increases step by step. Accordingly, the LM schedule travels slightly to the right. To compensate for this, the government reduces the fiscal expansion, thus shifting the IS schedule somewhat to the left. And so on. Once more, it remains an open question whether the stationary equilibrium is stable or not.

7.2.2. Investment Subsidy

As an alternative remedy, the government may cure an adverse shock in private investment by stimulating private investment directly. For instance, the government can grant investment subsidies or investment tax credits. In the current section, we return to bond finance of the budget deficit. More precisely, we consider an economy with fiscal policy, confer sections 5.3. and 6.2.

Essentially, the process of adjustment consists of two phases. At the start, let the economy be in the long-run equilibrium. All workers have got a job. Firms dispense with investment. The budget is balanced, and no public debt does exist. In the first phase, an investment shock comes about. Properly speaking, sales expectations deteriorate. For that reason, private investment becomes negative. In order to avoid this, the government subsidizes private investment at once. Hence output does not change, and full employment still prevails. Of course, the stock of capital is invariant. In addition, the investment subsidy gives rise to a budget deficit of equal amount.

In the second phase, sales expectations improve again. Therefore, private investment turns positive. To escape this, the government cancels the investment subsidy instantly. Output does not move, so the labour market continues to clear. The stock of capital is uniform, and the budget balances. The sum of the investment subsidies paid out during the first phase determines public debt.

Figure 1 illuminates the resulting time path. The autonomous decline in expected sales leads to a leftward shift of the IS curve. As a response, the government introduces an investment subsidy, thereby pushing the IS curve back to the right. Later on, the induced recovery in expected sales brings about a further rightward movement of the IS curve. On that ground, the government suspends the investment subsidy, thus pulling the IS curve back to its initial position.

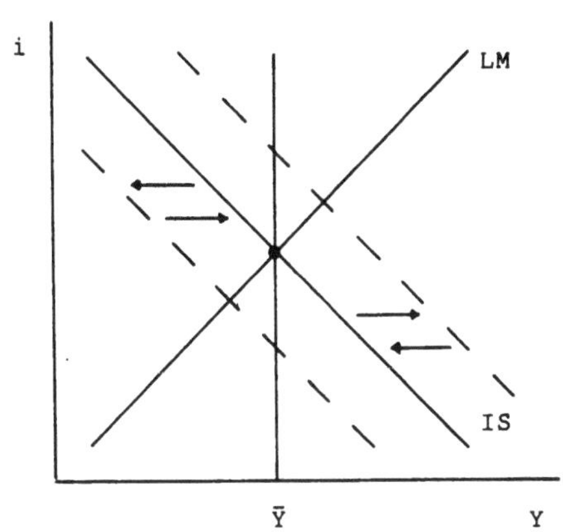

Figure 1. Investment Shock and Investment Subsidy.

During the first phase, unfortunately, the government has accumulated public debt. Then, during the second phase, public debt remained fixed. As a consequence, the government has to make interest payments on public debt. As time proceeds, this drives the stock of capital down to zero. Ultimately, the economy will collapse.

Last but not least, how does the investment subsidy perform as compared to public consumption? The investment subsidy, on the one hand, directly removes the cause of the disturbance. Government purchases, on the other hand, immediately affect aggregate demand. In this case, what is more, the budget tends to be balanced over the cycle.

7.2.3. Monetary Policy

In the present section, we shall outline monetary policy as an instrument to absorb an investment shock. Strictly speaking, the central bank augments the supply of money. This action lowers the rate of interest and hence advances private capital formation.

Here the short-run equilibrium can be characterized by a system of ten equations. As a starting point, consider equations (1) until (9) in section 6.2.2. Then substitute

(1) $$K^* = \frac{\alpha E}{i}$$

for (4) in section 6.2.2. In other words, the desired stock of capital is now influenced by the rate of interest as well. Besides, add the money market equation:

(2) $$M = \frac{kY}{i^{\eta}}$$

In terms of section 6.2.2., this is equation number ten. The right-hand side indicates the demand for money, where η symbolizes the interest elasticity.

In principle, the process of adjustment can be divided into two phases. At the beginning, the economy is in the long-run equilibrium. All workers find a job, whereas firms abstain from investment. The budget balances, and no public debt does exist. In the first phase, an investment shock emerges. More precisely, expected sales come down. Therefore, private investment becomes negative. In order to avert this, the central bank runs a monetary expansion. Output stays at the given level, thus full employment still prevails. The budget continues to balance, so there is no reason why public debt should build up.

In the second phase, expected sales go up again. On that account, private investment turns positive. To forestall this, the central bank switches over to a monetary contraction. More exactly, the central bank reduces the quantity of money to its initial value. Production stays put, hence the labour market keeps on clearing. The budget is always balanced, so no public debt comes into existence. As a result, monetary policy in fact succeeds, entailing no difficulties at all.

Figure 1 graphs the corresponding trajectory. The adverse investment shock displaces the IS schedule to the left. The central bank answers by a loose monetary policy, shifting the LM schedule to the right. In due course, sales expectations improve again, so the IS schedule returns to its original position. As a consequence, the central bank stops the monetary expansion. Accordingly, the LM schedule comes home, too.

The final point refers to a comparative evaluation of monetary policy versus fiscal policy. Above all, monetary policy seems to be much more easy. Moreover, it cures not the symptom but the cause. Government purchases, by way of contrast, directly affect aggregate demand. In addition, we have to keep in mind that different institutions are involved, the central bank and the government.

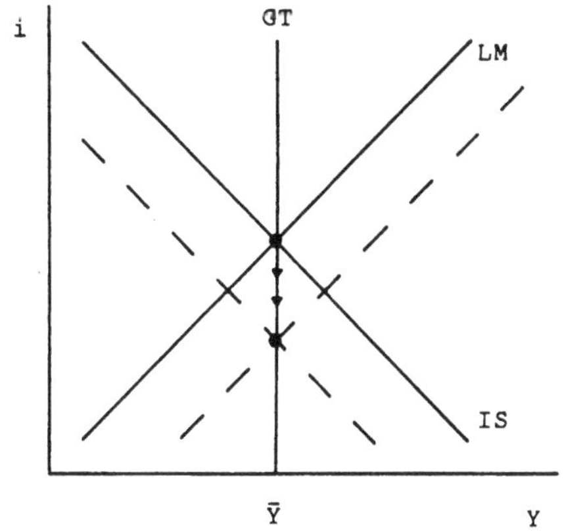

Figure 1. Investment Shock and Monetary Policy.

7.3. Monetary Shock

So far, in the present monograph, emphasis has been laid on an investment shock. Now, instead, a few words will be said on a monetary disturbance. However, a full-fledged model would be highly complex. That is why the associated problems will be sketched out only briefly. To begin with, in section 7.3.1., we shall look into the process of adjustment released by a monetary contraction. Then, in section 7.3.2., we shall explore how far fiscal policy is suited to fight a monetary shock. Finally, in section 7.3.3., we shall discuss monetary policy as an alternative instrument to overcome a monetary disturbance.

7.3.1. Process of Adjustment

First of all, to simplify matters, regard an economy without public sector. Here, the overlapping generations model will be extended to include money. Thus the long-run equilibrium can be expressed by a system of five equations:

(1) $$Y=K^{\alpha} N^{\beta}$$

(2) $$i=\frac{\alpha Y}{K}$$

(3) $$\frac{w}{P}=\frac{\beta Y}{N}$$

(4) $$\frac{M}{P}=\frac{kY}{i^{\eta}}$$

(5) $$i=\frac{\alpha}{\beta\delta}$$

Equation (4) states that the real supply of money corresponds to the real demand for money, confer e. g. section 4.3. Besides, (5) can be deduced by combining (2) with $K=\beta\delta Y$ from section 3.1.

The system (1) until (5) can be interpreted either as the steady state with flexible money wages or as the steady state with rigid money wages. Let us start with the long-run equilibrium under flexible money wages. In this case, $\alpha, \beta, \delta, \eta$, k, M and N are given exogenously, whereas i, w, K, P and Y are endogenous variables. There are as many equations as variables, so the system is determinate.

Now it is convenient to solve the model in terms of growth rates. (5) implies $\hat{i}=0$, where the hat denotes the rate of growth. In conjunction with (2), we arrive at $\hat{K}=\hat{Y}$. Beyond that, the production function can be written as $\hat{Y}=\alpha\hat{K}+\beta\hat{N}$. By virtue of $\hat{K}=\hat{Y}$ and $\hat{N}=0$, one can infer that $\hat{Y}=\alpha\hat{Y}$ and $\hat{Y}=0$. Likewise we obtain $\hat{K}=0$. Under these circumstances, (4) yields $\hat{P}=\hat{M}$. At last, (3) takes on the shape $\hat{w}=\hat{P}$ and $\hat{w}=\hat{M}$.

The outcome can be displayed in the following way:

(6) $$\hat{i}=\hat{K}=\hat{Y}=0$$

(7) $$\hat{w}=\hat{P}=\hat{M}$$

Consider, for instance, a one percent reduction in the quantity of money. Obviously, this disruption leaves no impact on interest rate, output and capital stock. As opposed to this, money wages and prices fall by one percent, too.

The next point refers to the long-run equilibrium under rigid money wages. In this case, $\alpha, \beta, \delta, \eta, k$, w and M are given exogenously, whereas i, K, N, P and Y

are endogenous variables. The number of equations matches the number of unknowns, hence the system is well defined. Once more, in terms of growth rates, (5) provides $\hat{i}=0$. Owing to that, (2) can be formulated as $\hat{K}=\hat{Y}$. Insert this into technology $\hat{Y}=\alpha\hat{K}+\beta\hat{N}$ to reach $\hat{Y}=\hat{N}$. Accordingly, one can deduce from (3) that $\hat{P}=0$. Against this background, (4) simplifies to $\hat{Y}=\hat{M}$.

These findings can be represented as follows:

$$\hat{K}=\hat{N}=\hat{Y}=\hat{M} \tag{8}$$

$$\hat{i}=\hat{P}=0 \tag{9}$$

For example, a one percent decline in the quantity of money lowers the stock of capital, labour demand and output by one percent. On the other hand, this shock has no influence on the rate of interest and on prices. These results are in remarkable constrast to the conclusions drawn for flexible money wages.

Having laid this foundation, we are in a position to depict the process of adjustment in a stylized way. Initially, the economy is in the steady state with flexible money wages. In this situation, a monetary disturbance happens. As a consequence, the economy passes through the steady state with rigid money wages, eventually settling down in the steady state with flexible money wages.

In a sense, the process of adjustment can be split up into two phases. At the beginning, the economy is in the stationary equilibrium with flexible money wages. All workers have got a job, and firms refrain from investment. In the first phase, a monetary disruption comes about. More precisely, the quantity of money contracts spontaneously. In the stationary equilibrium with rigid money wages, firms do not invest. Both autonomous consumption and output have dropped to a lower level. Similarly, firms have been compelled to dismiss some workers. And the stock of capital has also been reduced. During the process of adjustment, the rate of interest moved at a higher plane. For that time, private investment became negative, so autonomous consumption and output diminished step by step.

At this juncture, we turn to the second phase. In the stationary equilibrium with flexible money wages, money wages and prices have been revised downwards. Therefore, real balances have returned to their original value. Firms dispense with investment. Both autonomous consumption and output have come back to their starting point. Again, firms engage all workers. And the stock of capital has been replenished. During the process of adjustment, the rate of interest moved at a lower level. Temporarily, private investment became positive, thus autonomous consumption and output increased round by round.

Figure 1 explains the cyclical adjustment induced by a monetary shock. The initial diminution in the quantity of money leads to a leftward displacement of the LM curve. Private investment turns negative and autonomous consumption declines, hence the IS curve shifts to the left, too. As time goes on, prices begin to fall, thereby augmenting real balances. In the diagram, the LM curve travels back to the right. Private investment becomes positive and automomous consumption rises, so the IS curve follows up.

At last, a few words will be said on an economy with public sector. In figure 1, a monetary contraction pushes the LM schedule to the left. Because of that, the budget gets into a deficit. Over time, public debt will build up, ultimately tending to explode. This in turn will squeeze the stock of capital down to zero. To conclude, a long-run equilibrium does indeed exist. Unfortunately, however, it proves to be unstable.

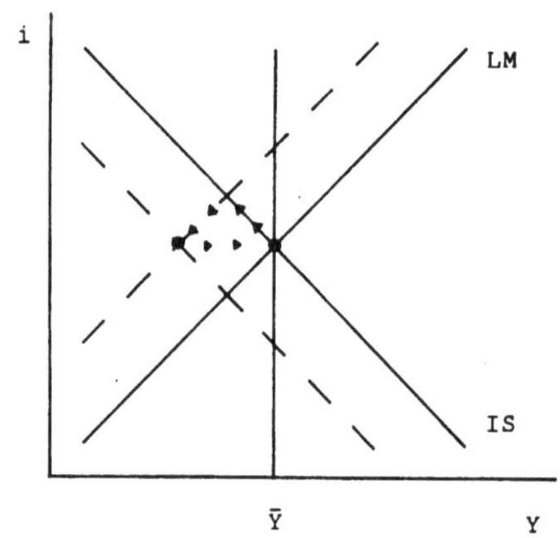

Figure 1. Monetary Shock and Cyclical Adjustment.

7.3.2. Fiscal Policy

In the current section, we shall discuss whether fiscal policy is suited to absorb a monetary shock. The forthcoming analysis will be based on the model set out in the previous section.

At the beginning, in period 0, the economy is in the long-run equilibrium. Especially, all workers have got a job. Firms abstain from investment. The budget balances, and no public debt does exist. Under these circumstances, in period 1, a monetary shock occurs. More precisely, the quantity of money diminishes spontaneously. Owing to that, private investment turns negative. In order to prevent unemployment, the government raises public consumption immediately. Therefore, output does not change. For the time being, the stock of capital is invariant. The increase in government purchases brings the budget into deficit, yet there is still no public debt.

Then, in period 2, the quantity of money stays at the lower level. Accordingly, private investment remains negative. To protect full employment, the government keeps public consumption at the higher level. Of course, output does not react. Further, the negative investment contributes to a reduction in the stock of capital. The budget continues to be in deficit, so public debt builds up. This process recurs period by period.

Figure 1 visualizes the process of adjustment. Initially, the economy is in the steady state. Then a monetary contraction emerges, shifting the LM schedule to the left. The government answers by a fiscal expansion. In the diagram, both the IS schedule and the GT vertical move to the right. As time proceeds, however, public debt tends to explode, which fatally crowds out the stock of capital. At the end, the economy must break down.

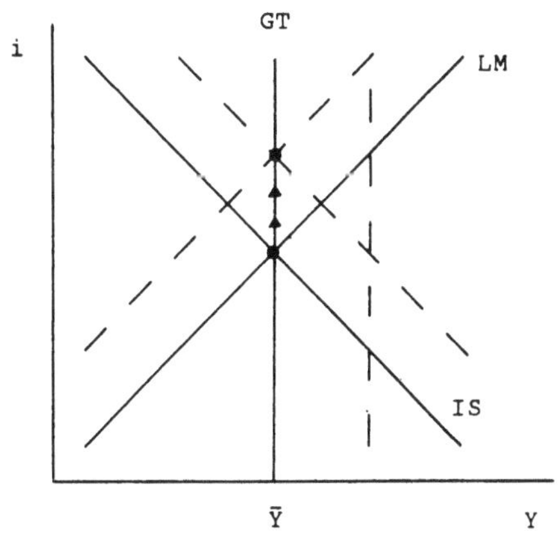

Figure 1. Monetary Shock and Fiscal Policy.

7.3.3. Monetary Policy

In the current section, we shall examine how far monetary policy is qualified to overcome a monetary disturbance.

At the start, in period 0, the economy is in the stationary equilibrium. Above all, the labour market clears. Firms refrain from investment. The budget is balanced, and no public debt does exist. Against this background, in period 1, a monetary disruption takes place, throwing the economy out of equilibrium. Strictly speaking, the quantity of money comes down autonomously. On that account, private investment turns negative. To avoid this, the central bank switches over to a loose monetary policy. That is to say, the central bank lifts the quantity of money back to its original level. As a consequence, the shock leaves no impact on output and employment. Besides, the stock of capital is uniform. The budget still balances, and there is no public debt. In summary, this strategy involves no problem.

Figure 1 graphs how the economy develops over time. At the outset, the economy is in the long-run equilibrium. Then the exogenous monetary contraction leads to a leftward shift of the LM curve. As a response, the endogenous monetary expansion brings the LM curve back to the right until it reaches its starting point. By the way, the GT line stays put.

Finally, we shall confront monetary policy and fiscal policy with one another. Fiscal policy, on the one hand, has a direct influence on aggregate demand. But ultimately it drives the stock of capital down to zero, so the economy will collapse. Monetary policy, on the other hand, cures the cause of the disease, hence no problem will be left.

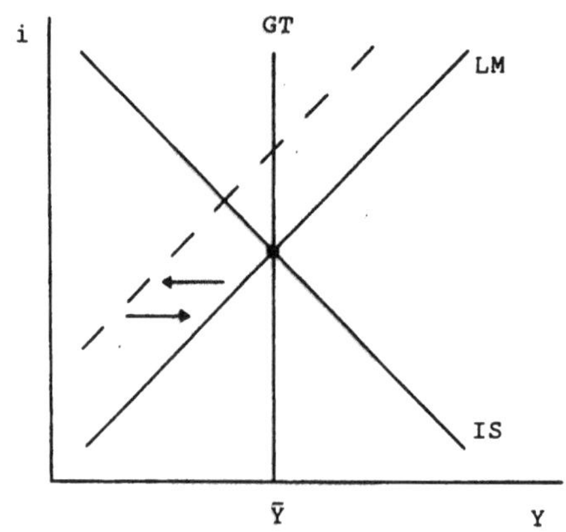

Figure 1. Monetary Shock and Monetary Policy.

7.4. Growing Economy

So far, the focus was on a stationary economy. Now, instead, we shall address a growing economy. To begin with, in section 7.4.1., we shall concentrate on primary budget deficits. In a stationary economy, a tax cut gives rise to fatal crowding out. Does this hold in a growing economy, too? Then, in section 7.4.2., the optimum of fiscal policy will be determined. In a stationary economy, the budget should be balanced across the cycle. In a growing economy, as opposed to that, should the government run a budget deficit or a budget surplus over the cycle as a whole?

7.4.1. Fiscal Policy

Suppose that the government, starting form a balanced budget, reduces the tax rate forever. In a stationary economy, as a consequence, public debt tends to explode. This, in turn, squeezes the stock of capital down to zero, as has been demonstrated above. Eventually, the economy will break down. Does this apply to a growing economy, too?

In answering this question, it proves useful to distinguish between primary and secondary budget deficits. A secondary budget deficit is identical to net public borrowing, see above. In addition, a primary budget deficit is defined as the excess of net public borrowing over the interest payments on public debt. A good deal of analysis has been performed on secondary budget deficits. The papers by e.g. Diamond (1965) and Phelps and Shell (1969) have well established that secondary budget deficits are feasible in the long run. Primary budget deficits, on the other hand, seem to be an almost neglected field of research. Can primary budget deficits be sustained? Put another way, can the government in the long run spend more on goods and services than it receives by taxation?

If the interest rate falls short of the growth rate, then primary budget deficits indeed are feasible in the long run. Conversely, if the interest rate exceeds the growth rate, then primary budget deficits cannot be sustained, as is well known (e.g. Sargent and Wallace 1981). The interest rate, however, is endogenous. One must expect that primary budget deficits push up the interest rate. This raises the question whether the interest rate can really stay below the growth rate.

Carlberg (1983, 1988) studies a Solow growth model with a proportional saving function. He reaches the conclusion that as a rule the government cannot run a primary budget deficit perpetually. Tobin (1986) investigates a lifecycle growth model, adopting phase-diagram techniques. There the focus is on the long-run implications of the monetary-fiscal mix. Numerical simulations suggest that primary budget deficits may well end in catastrophes. However, Tobin offers no clearcut feasibility condition. The current section is based on an overlapping generations model of a growing economy (cf. Michaelis 1989). Explicitly, the feasibility condition will be derived and evaluated. It will be argued that primary budget deficits generally cannot be sustained.

The analysis will be carried out within the following basic framework. Private firms produce a homogeneous commodity Y by means of private capital K and labour N. Properly speaking, N denotes the number of active workers. For ease of exposition, consider a Cobb-Douglas technology showing constant returns to scale:

(1) $$Y = K^{\alpha} N^{\beta}$$

with $\alpha > 0$, $\beta > 0$ and $\alpha + \beta = 1$. There is full employment of capital and labour. Output Y can be devoted to private consumption C, private investment I and public consumption G:

(2) $$Y = C + I + G$$

Let labour grow at the natural rate:

(3) $$\hat{N} = n = \text{const}$$

Firms maximize profits

$$\Pi = Y - iK - wN \tag{4}$$

under perfect competition, so the interest rate corresponds to the marginal product of capital:

$$i = \frac{\partial Y}{\partial K} = \frac{\alpha Y}{K} \tag{5}$$

Analogously, the wage rate equals the marginal product of labour:

$$w = \frac{\partial Y}{\partial N} = \frac{\beta Y}{N} \tag{6}$$

The government raises loans and collects a tax to finance both public consumption and the interest payments on public debt. The government buys a given fraction $g = \text{const.}$ of national product:

$$G = gY \tag{7}$$

Moreover, the government imposes a tax T at the flat rate $t =$ const. on labour income:

$$T = t\beta Y \tag{8}$$

Under a general income tax, principally the same results obtain even though the analysis becomes more complex. Specifically, we assume that the government wishes to spend more on public consumption than it receives by taxation: $G > T$. For this reason, the government runs a primary budget deficit

$$H := G - T \tag{9}$$

Accordingly, the primary deficit ratio is

$$h := g - \beta t \tag{10}$$

D_τ stands for public debt issued in period $\tau - 1$ and retired in period τ. The government pays the interest rate i on public debt D, so public interest amounts to iD. The government sells new bonds in order to cover the primary budget deficit, to redeem old bonds, and to pay interest on them:

$$D_{+1} = H + D + iD \tag{11}$$

This is the government budget constraint. The secondary budget deficit is identical to net public borrowing: $D_{+1} - D = H + iD$. Evidently, a primary budget deficit always implies a secondary budget deficit: $D_{+1} - D > H$. Of course, a secondary budget deficit without a primary budget deficit is sustainable. But unfortunately it means that taxation exceeds public consumption.

In the steady state, public debt builds up at the natural rate:

(12) $$D_{+1} = (1+n)D$$

The interest rate can be written as $i = \alpha / v$, where $v := K / Y$ represents the capital-output ratio. Further, it is convenient to introduce the debt-capital ratio $d := D / K$. Now substitute $D_{+1} = (1+n)D$, $i = \alpha / v$ and $d := D / K$ into $D_{+1} = H + D + iD$ and solve for

(13) $$v = \frac{h + \alpha d}{dn}$$

The individual lifecycle is composed of two periods, of the working period and of the retirement period. During the working period, the individual receives labour income, which he partly cosumes and partly saves. The savings are used to buy government bonds and private bonds. During the retirement period, the individual earns interest on the bonds and sells the bonds altogether. The proceeds are entirely consumed, no bequests are left.

The utility u of the representative individual depends on private consumption per head in the working period c^1 and on private consumption per head in the retirement period c^2. Take a logarithmic utility function:

(14) $$u = \gamma \log c^1 + \delta \log c^2$$

with $\gamma > 0$, $\delta > 0$ and $\gamma + \delta = 1$. Without losing generality, we postulate that public consumption does not affect intertemporal allocation. That is to say, public consumption does not enter the utility function explicitly.

The budget constraint of the representative individual covers the whole lifecycle. $(1-t)w$ is net labour income in the working period and $(1-t)w - c^1$ are private savings in the working period. The individual earns the interest rate i on private savings, so private consumption in the retirement period is $[(1-t)w - c^1](1+i) = c^2$. As a consequence, the individual budget constraint can be stated as:

(15) $$c^1 + \frac{c^2}{1+i} = (1-t)w$$

The individual chooses present and future consumption so as to maximize utility subject to its budget constraint. The evaluation of the Lagrange function yields private consumption per head in the working period:

$$c^1 = \gamma(1-t)w \tag{16}$$

Net labour income minus private consumption per head gives private savings per head $s=(1-t)w-c^1$ or

$$s=\delta(1-t)w \tag{17}$$

The private savings of the active generation amount to $S=sN$. Observe (6) and (17) to obtain:

$$S=\beta\delta(1-t)Y \tag{18}$$

The private savings of the working generation serve to finance public debt and private capital of the subsequent period:

$$D_{+1}+K_{+1}=S \tag{19}$$

In the steady state, private capital accumulates at the natural rate:

$$K_{+1}=(1+n)K \tag{20}$$

Now insert (12), (18) and (20) into (19), taking account of $v:=K/Y$ and $d:=D/K$:

$$v=\frac{\beta\delta(1-t)}{(1+d)(1+n)} \tag{21}$$

The debt-capital ratio d proves to be a strategic variable, as will be demonstrated next. Equate (13) and (21), then solve this quadratic equation for d:

$$d=-\frac{(\alpha+h)(1+n)-\beta\delta n(1-t)}{2\alpha(1+n)} \pm\sqrt{\frac{[(\alpha+h)(1+n)-\beta\delta n(1-t)]^2}{[2\alpha(1+n)]^2}-\frac{h}{\alpha}} \tag{22}$$

The reduced discriminant $A=[(\alpha+h)(1+n)-\beta\delta n(1-t)]^2-4\alpha(1+n)^2h$ of (22) vanishes at:

$$h_{1,2}=\frac{\alpha(1+n)+\beta\delta n(1-t)}{1+n}$$

$$\mp\sqrt{\frac{4\alpha\beta\delta n(1-t)}{1+n}} \tag{23}$$

The close inspection of (23) reveals that h_1 and h_2 are both real and positive with $h_1 < h_2$ (see appendix to the current section).

d, in turn, is real and positive if and only if:

$$\delta > \frac{\alpha(1+n)}{\beta n(1-t)} \quad \text{and } h \leq h_1 \tag{24}$$

(see appendix). In other words, a steady state of growth does exist if and only if the elasticity of future consumption is high and the primary deficit ratio is low. As a result, this is the necessary and sufficient condition for primary budget deficits to be sustainable.

To illustrate this condition, consider a numerical example with $\alpha = 0.2$ and $t = 0.2$. The working period and the retirement period each take 30 years. Let labour grow at an annual rate of 3%, which implies $n = 1.427$. According to (24), the critical level of the future consumption elasticity is 0.531. Further, according to (23), the critical level of the primary deficit ratio is a function of the future consumption elasticity:

δ	h_1
0.1	0
0.2	0
0.3	0
0.4	0
0.5	0
0.6	0.0008
0.7	0.0044

If the future consumption elasticity is 0.4 or 0.5, the critical value of the primary deficit ratio is 0. In this situation, primary budget deficits cannot be sustained. If the future consumption elasticity is 0.6, the critical value of the primary deficit ratio amounts to 0.0008. In this situation, two different cases may occur. If the primary deficit ratio falls short of 0.0008, primary budget deficits in fact are feasible. Conversely, if the primary deficit ratio exceeds 0.0008, primary budget deficits again are not feasible. However, $\delta > 0.5$ requires a negative rate of time preference. What is more, if α rises or n falls, the critical level of δ becomes even larger.

Empirical evidence seems to suggest that primary budget deficits generally cannot be sustained (e.g. Barth, Russek and Iden 1986, Hamilton and Flavin 1986). On the other hand, there may be an exception to this rule. If both the rate of time preference and the primary deficit ratio are extremely low, then primary budget deficits indeed are feasible in the long run. In summary, primary budget deficits are unlikely to be sustainable.

Now imagine a situation, where primary budget deficits cannot be sustained (i.e. $\delta \leq \alpha(1+n)/[\beta n(1-t)]$ or $h > h_1$). What happens if the government nevertheless runs a primary budget deficit? Suppose that the government, starting from budget equilibrium, reduces the tax rate. Obviously, the tax cut forces the government to raise loans. First of all, public borrowing crowds out private investment and discourages capital formation. Moreover, public borrowing leads to the accumulation of public debt. In addition, the interest rate is bid up as capital becomes scarce. Both factors contribute to a rise in public interest. In order to cover this, the government must raise even more loans.

As a consequence, private investment and capital formation slow down once again. The economy ends up in a vicious circle where the government borrows to finance the interest payments on public debt. As soon as public borrowing completely absorbs private savings, private investment becomes negative. That is to say, worn-out machines are no longer replaced. The stock of capital begins to decline, while labour continues to grow. This curbs the expansion of output. Ultimately, the stock of capital will be exhausted, thus stopping all economic activities.

The basic theorem has some far-reaching consequences. 1) If the interest rate stays below the growth rate, then primary budget deficits are feasible in the long run, as is well known (e.g. Sargent and Wallace 1981). But the basic theorem implies that under primary budget deficits the interest rate surpasses the growth rate, so primary budget deficits cannot be sustained. 2) In the long run, the government cannot spend more on goods and services than it receives by taxation. The reason is that the interest payments on public debt exceed public borrowing. 3) A reduction of the tax rate, starting from a balanced budget, eventually drives capital and output down to zero.

4) Does fiscal policy matter? This question was raised by Blinder and Solow (1973) and resumed by Tobin and Buiter (1976). The short-run effects can be traced in an elaborate IS-LM model, whereas the long-run effects are given by the present model. Here the long run is characterized by the fact that wages, prices and capital have adjusted appropriately. Now the basic theorem states that a fiscal expansion crowds out private investment to such an extent that the economy will break down in the long-run. As a fundamental result, this confirms the conclusions drawn for a stationary economy.

At first sight, the basic theorem is in sharp contrast to the Ricardian equivalence theorem. Barro (1974) examined an overlapping generations model with bequests. Within this framework, debt finance is equivalent to tax finance. Strictly speaking, secondary budget deficits do not matter. Primary budget deficits, however, again are not feasible in the long-run.

Appendix

The discriminant of (23) is positive, so h_1 and h_2 are real. Further h_1 is positive, since $[\alpha(1+n)-\beta\delta n(1-t)]^2$ is positive. Therefore, h_1 and h_2 are real and positive.

Evidently (22) can be written as $d=-P/Q\pm\sqrt{R}$. In addition, the reduced discriminant of (22) can be stated as $A=(h-h_1)(h-h_2)$. This gives rise to four cases. First, if $h_1<h<h_2$, then $A<0$. Second, if $h\leq h_1$ and $\delta<\alpha(1+n)/[\beta n(1-t)]$, then $A\geq 0$ and $d<0$. Proof: P is positive. Now square $\sqrt{R}<P/Q$ to confirm $d<0$. Third, if $h\leq h_1$ and $\delta>\alpha(1+n)/[\beta n(1-t)]$, then $A\geq 0$ and $d>0$. In this case, P is negative. Next square $-P/Q>\sqrt{R}$ to verify $d>0$. Fourth, if $h\geq h_2$, then $A\geq 0$ and $d<0$. Proof: Here P is positive. Finally square $\sqrt{R}<P/Q$ to see $d<0$.

7.4.2. Optimum Fiscal Policy

As a baseline, take a stationary economy. Suppose that the government, starting from a budget equilibrium, reduces the tax rate forever. In the long-run, as a consequence, public debt tends to explode, thereby driving the stock of capital down to zero. Against this background, the optimum fiscal policy seems to be to balance the budget. In the short-run, what is more, the government should equilibrate the budget across the cycle. Does this apply to a growing economy, too? Should the government run a budget deficit or a budget surplus over the cycle as a whole?

To simplify matters, the current section rests on a Solow growth model with a proportional saving function (cf. Carlberg 1983, 1988). Principally the same results can be obtained for an overlapping generations model (Michaelis 1989) and for a Ramsey model of optimum growth (Grill 1989).

Firms manufacture a single commodity Y with the help of private capital K and labour N. For ease of exposition, consider a Cobb-Douglas technology exhibiting constant returns to scale:

(1) $$Y=K^{\alpha}N^{\beta}$$

with $\alpha>0$, $\beta>0$ and $\alpha+\beta=1$. It prevails full employment of private capital and labour. Output Y can be dedicated to private consumption C, to private investment I and to public consumption G:

(2) $$Y=C+I+G$$

The government raises loans and levies an income tax. It pays the interest rate i on public debt D, so public interest amounts to iD. (Net) public borrowing B

and tax revenue T serve to cover both public consumption G and public interest iD. Accordingly, the government budget constraint is

(3) $$B+T=G+iD$$

The government buys a given fraction $g=$ const. of national product:

(4) $$G=gY$$

Moreover, the government borrows a fixed share $b=$ const. of national income:

(5) $$B=bY$$

Public borrowing, in turn, enhances public debt:

(6) $$\dot{D}=B$$

Here the dot denotes the time derivative.

Factor income and debt income, net after tax respectively, make up disposable income

(7) $$Y_d=Y+iD-T$$

Insert $iD-T=B-G=bY-gY$ to express disposable income in terms of factor income:

(8) $$Y_d=(1+b-g)Y$$

If $b \lesseqgtr g$, then $Y_d \lesseqgtr Y$. That means, under a low (high) borrowing ratio, disposable income falls short of (exceeds) factor income.

Households save a certain proportion $s=$ const. of disposable income:

(9) $$S=sY_d$$

A good deal of private savings is absorbed by public borrowing, the remainder being left for private investment

(10) $$I=S-B$$

Private investment, in turn, augments the stock of private capital:

(11) $$\dot{K}=I$$

This furnishes $\dot{K} = I = S - B = s(1 + b - g)\,Y - bY$. Thus the growth rate of private capital is influenced by the private saving ratio s, by the public borrowing ratio b, by the public consumption ratio g, and by the capital coefficient

(12) $$\hat{K} = \frac{s(1 + b - g) - b}{v}$$

with capital coefficient $v := K / Y$. Let labour develop at the natural rate

(13) $$\hat{N} = n = \text{const.}$$

In the steady state, private capital builds up at the natural rate:

(14) $$n = \frac{s(1 + b - g) - b}{v}$$

Here, b, g, n and s are constant, whereas v can adapt itself.

The analysis of (14) reveals that if $b \lesseqgtr (s - gs)/(1 - s)$, then $v \gtreqless 0$. In other words, if the public borrowing ratio is low compared to the private saving ratio, the capital coefficient is positive. On the other hand, if the public borrowing ratio surpasses a critical level, the capital coefficient becomes negative, which economically makes no sense. To illustrate this, consider a numerical example with $g = 0.2$ and $s = 0.1$. If $b \lesseqgtr 0.09$, then $v \gtreqless 0$. That is to say, if the government raises loans in excess of 9% of national income, capital formation will cease altogether.

Speaking more generally, a rise in the public borrowing ratio lowers the capital coefficient, as can be seen from equation (14). What is the explanation for this effect? Evidently, two counteracting forces are at work. On the one hand, the increase in public borrowing crowds out private investment, thereby reducing capital formation. On the other hand, the increase in public borrowing enhances public debt, while the reduction of capital formation drives up the interest rate. Both factors contribute to an expansion of public interest, disposable income, private savings and capital formation. On balance, the first channel is much more important than the second.

In summary, a steady state of growth indeed exists, provided that the public borrowing ratio is sufficiently small. Private capital, labour, income, public borrowing, public debt, tax revenue and public consumption expand at the natural rate: $\hat{K} = \hat{N} = \hat{Y} = \hat{B} = \hat{D} = \hat{T} = \hat{G} = n$.

So far the public borrowing ratio was assumed to be given arbitrarily. Now we shall try to find out the optimal borrowing ratio. Here the natural criterion for efficiency is the sum of private and public consumption per head. Strictly speaking, which public borrowing ratio maximizes the sum of private and public consumption per head $z = C/N + G/N$?

Output per head $y = Y/N$ is a familiar function $y = k^{\alpha}$ of capital per head $k = K/N$. Restate $C + G = Y - I = Y - nK$ as $z = y - nk$. Then differentiate z for k, set the derivative equal to zero and rearrange: $dy/dk = n$. From this one can infer $(dy/dk)\,(k/y) = n\,(k/y)$ and $\alpha = nv$. Finally substitute $\alpha = nv$ into (14) and solve for b:

(15) $$b^* = \frac{s - gs - \alpha}{1 - s}$$

As a result, the optimal borrowing ratio b^* depends on the private saving ratio s, on the public consumption ratio g, and on technology α.

This has some far-reaching consequences for the government budget constraint $B + T = G + iD$, as will be proved next. The combination of $i = dy/dk$ and $dy/dk = n$ yields:

(16) $$i = n$$

Insert this into $B = \dot{D} = nD$ to arrive at

(17) $$B = iD \text{ and } T = G$$

Hence, the interest payments on public debt exactly equal public borrowing. But this does not mean that public debt is redundant. On the contrary, public borrowing is needed to control capital formation.

Actually, public debt only exists when public borrowing is positive. The analysis of (15) reveals:

(18) $$\text{If } s \gtrless \alpha/(1-g), \quad \text{then } b^* \gtrless 0$$

In other words, if the private saving ratio is high (low) as compared to the private capital elasticity and the public consumption ratio, the optimal borrowing ratio is positive (negative). Under a high saving ratio, the government should indeed raise loans in order to prevent excessive capital formation. Conversely, under a low saving ratio, the government should lend money to the private sector in order to stimulate capital formation.

To illustrate this condition, consider a numerical example with $\alpha = 0.2$, $s = 0.1$ and $g = 0.2$. According to (15), the optimal borrowing ratio is $b^* = -0.13$. In this situation, optimum public debt is negative. With a national income of 100, expenditures and revenue are as follows. The government buys goods and services 20 and makes loans to the private sector 13. On the other hand, the government imposes a tax 20 and receives interest payments on public assets 13. Speaking more generally, if the private saving ratio exceeds (falls short of) 0.25, the government should be a debtor (creditor).

We turn now to the tax rate which is required to balance the budget. The government levies a tax at the flat rate $t = \text{const.}$ on both factor income and debt income:

(19) $$T = t\,(Y + iD)$$

The golden rule of public debt implies $T = G = gY$ and $iD = B = bY$. Put this into (19) and solve for $t = g/(1+b)$. This together with (15) provides the optimal tax rate:

(20) $$t^* = \frac{g - gs}{\beta - gs}$$

In the numerical example, the tax rate is $t^* = 0.23$.

What does this suggest for the conduct of fiscal policy in the short run? Evidently, it is useful to distinguish two cases, depending on the size of the private saving ratio. If the private saving ratio is large, the government should run a budget deficit over the cycle as a whole. Now imagine that an investment shock occurs. In the first phase, to fight underemployment, the government has even to increase the budget deficit. In the second phase, to avoid overemployment, the government has to reduce the budget deficit well below the initial level.

Conversely, if the private saving ratio is small, the government should strive for a budget surplus across the cycle. Suppose again that an investment shock happens. In the first phase, as a response, the government must cut down the budget surplus. In the second phase, on the other hand, the government must raise the budget surplus clearly above the average level.

This outcome is in remarkable contrast to the conclusions drawn for a stationary economy. There, the government should balance the budget over the cycle. In the first phase, the government ought to run a budget deficit. Then, in the second phase, it ought to switch over to a budget surplus.

If you want a high-investment, rapid-growth society, reverse the drift of fiscal and monetary policy. Over the business cycle as a whole, aim for budget surpluses. Turn more of the economy's cyclical management over to the Fed. Make sure that Congress resists the temptation to boost spending or cut taxes in recessions, and make sure that the Fed reacts as quickly to unemployment as it does to inflation.

Paul A. Samuelson
William D. Nordhaus

8. Conclusion

The present study is concerned with the short-run and long-run effects of fiscal policy on employment, output and prices. Suppose that an investment shock causes unemployment. Then it is the task of fiscal policy to restore full employment in the short run. This goes along with a budget deficit which adds to public debt. Here a number of questions arise: What are the long-run consequences of the fiscal expansion? Will public debt tend to explode? Will the stock of capital ultimately shrink back to zero? In other words, will there be fatal crowding out?

Fiscal policy induces various processes of adjustment which run at different speeds. This fact has been modelled here by distinguishing between the short-run equilibrium and the long-run equilibrium. That is to say, in the short period only the fast variables accommodate, while in the long-period the slow variables accommodate too. Properly speaking, in the short term money wages are rigid. The stock of capital and public debt are given exogenously. Technology is characterized by fixed coefficients since substitution is a slow process. In the long term, however, money wages are flexible. The stock of capital and public debt adapt themselves appropriately. The production function is smooth.

The basic exposition of the present monograph is as follows. At first, in chapters 2 and 3, we introduced the short-run and the long-run equilibrium. Then, in chapter 4, the process of adjustment linking the short-run and the long-run equilibrium was sketched out briefly. What is more, in chapters 5 and 6, we argued that an investment shock generates a cyclical process of adjustment. This in turn requires a cyclical path of fiscal policy. As a fundamental result, the budget will be balanced over the cycle as a whole. Finally, in chapter 7, the standard model was extended in several directions.

To begin with, in chapter 2, we inaugurated the short-run equilibrium. In the short period, money wages are sticky. The stock of capital and public debt are given exogenously. Technology is characterized by fixed coefficients, since substitution is a slow process. The analysis was carried out within the familiar setting of the IS-LM model. Aggregate supply was assumed to be perfectly elastic, so output is determined by aggregate demand.

Initially, full employment prevails, and the budget is balanced. In this situation, an investment shock occurs. Properly speaking, sales expectations deteriorate, thus autonomous investment declines. This compels firms to reduce output and to lay off workers. As a consequence, unemployment emerges. The fall in income goes along with a fall in tax revenue, hence the budget gets into deficit. In order to restore full employment, the government answers by a fiscal expansion. That is to say, the government buys more goods and services, thereby raising output. Further, the increase in government purchases aggravates the budget deficit.

Then, in chapter 3, we discussed the long-run equilibrium. In the long period, money wages are flexible. The stock of capital and public debt adjust themselves appropriately. The production function is smooth. The investigation was based on an overlapping generations model without bequests. Chapter 3 offered the real analysis of a stationary economy.

Now imagine that the government pursues a loose fiscal policy. More precisely, suppose that the government steps up public consumption. The accompanying budget deficit contributes to the accumulation of public debt. This displaces private capital, so output comes down. The associated diminution in private savings reinforces the diminution in private capital and output. The rate of interest rises, as capital becomes scarce. This together with the growth of public debt enhances public interest.

In order to cover this, the government must raise even more loans. Therefore, the economy enters a vicious circle where the government borrows in order to finance the interest payments on public debt. In the long run, public debt tends to explode, which drives the stock of capital down to zero. There will be fatal crowding out, hence ultimately the economy must break down.

Here the question arises whether this process can be cured. Three possible solutions have been examined. First, the government brings public consumption down to its initial value. And second, the government stabilizes public debt at its current level. Under both strategies, nevertheless, the stock of capital eventually shrinks back to zero. Third, the government retires public debt altogether. Only in this case, the government succeeds in reestablishing equilibrium. In a sense, public debt is like a killer virus. It breeds itself and displaces all other activities.

In the short run, a fiscal expansion lifts output. In the long run, however, it squeezes output down to zero. Against this background, in chapter 4, we briefly sketched out the process of adjustment linking the short-term and the long-term equilibrium. At the start, let the economy move in the steady state. All workers have got a job. Firms abstain from investment, so the stock of capital does not change. The budget is balanced, and there is no public debt.

Under these circumstances, suddenly, an investment shock takes place. Sales expectations worsen, hence private investment drops spontaneously. In order to keep up full employment, the government raises public consumption. In the short-run equilibrium, the labour market clears. Private investment is negative, and the budget shows a deficit.

As time goes on, in the medium run, the budget deficit builds up public debt round by round. The subsequent growth of public interest propels disposable income, private consumption and aggregate demand. Because the economy hits against full employment, money wages and prices begin to rise, thereby lowering real balances. On that account, the rate of interest springs up. This together with the accumulation of public debt augments public interest. In order to cover this, the government enlarges the budget deficit, thus speeding up the growth of public debt.

What is more, the boost of the interest rate further depresses private investment. Strictly speaking, private investment becomes even more negative. Accordingly, the stock of capital and capacity output diminish step by step. By the way, the ensuing fall in income leads to a fall in tax proceeds, which again elevates the budget deficit and public debt. In the long run, public debt is inclined to blow up. This, in turn, drives the stock of capital down to zero. At the end, the economy will collapse.

In the short term, a loose fiscal policy increases output, as has been mentioned above. In the long term, on the other hand, output shrinks back to zero. Judging from this, the long-term cost of fiscal policy seems to be forbidding. This brings up the issue whether the analysis presented so far is really adequate. Therefore, in chapters 5 and 6, it has been argued instead that an investment shock induces a cyclical process of adjustment. This, in turn, requires a cyclical path of fiscal policy. As a major result, the budget will be balanced over the cycle as a whole.

To begin with, in section 5.1., we considered an economy without public sector. The investigation rests on an extended multiplier-accelerator model of a stationary economy. In principle, the process of adjustment can be divided into two phases. Initially, the economy reproduces itself in the long-run equilibrium. All workers have got a job. Firms refrain from investment, so the stock of capital does not vary.

In the first phase, sales expectations deteriorate exogenously. For that reason, businesses postpone the replacement of capital. Private investment becomes negative, thus the stock of capital declines round by round. As a consequence, unemployment comes into existence.

In the second phase, sales expectations recover endogenously. Owing to that, enterprises make good the replacement of capital. Private investment turns positive, thereby replenishing the stock of capital. Now the economy suffers from overemployment. In the long run, again all workers find a job. Firms do no longer invest, hence the stock of capital is uniform. What is more, the steady state after disturbance coincides with the steady state before disturbance.

In summary, the investment shock generates a cyclical process of adjustment. In addition, the long-run equilibrium proves to be stable.

Then, in section 6.1., the public sector has been incorporated into the model. There, the government adheres to a passive fiscal policy. Essentially, the process of adjustment consists of two phases. At the start, the economy is in the stationary equilibrium. The labour market clears. Firms dispense with investment, so the stock of capital does not alter. The budget is balanced, and there is no public debt.

In the first phase, abruptly, expected sales worsen. As a response, private investment becomes negative, thus lowering the stock of capital. On that ground, unemployment emerges. The reduction in income goes along with a reduction in tax earnings. The budget gets into deficit, accordingly public debt begins to accumulate.

In the second phase, expected sales improve again. Private investment turns positive, which enhances the stock of capital. By virtue of that, overemployment arises. The increase in income causes an increase in tax proceeds. The budget moves into surplus, so public debt is being paid off. But in the long run, public debt tends to explode. As a consequence, this squeezes the stock of capital down to zero. Put differently, there will be fatal crowding out.

To conclude, the investment shock leads to a cyclical process of adjustment. However, the budget will not be balanced across the cycle as a whole. In this situation, the long-run equilibrium proves to be unstable. Ultimately, the economy must break down.

Finally, in section 6.2., we postulated that the government pursues an active fiscal policy. Once more, the process of adjustment can be split up into two phases. Initially, the economy is in the steady state. In particular, all workers have got a job. Businesses abstain from investment, so the stock of capital remains unchanged. The budget is balanced, and there is no public debt.

In the first phase, expected sales drop arbitrarily. Private investment turns negative, hence the stock of capital dwindles away. In order to prevent unemployment from coming into existence, the government expands public consumption. This brings the budget into deficit, thus augmenting public debt.

In the second phase, expected sales spring up again. Private investment turns positive, which fills up the stock of capital. To avoid overemployment, the government contracts public consumption. The budget switches over into surplus, thereby redeeming public debt. Yet in the long run, public debt is liable to grow without limits. Due to that, the stock of capital shrinks back to zero. In other words, there will be fatal crowding out.

To sum up, the investment shock induces a cyclical process of adjustment. This in turn calls for a cyclical path of fiscal policy. Unfortunately, however, the budget will not be balanced over the cycle as a whole. Again, the long-run equilibrium proves to be unstable. Eventually, the economy must collapse.

This raises the problem whether the government can restore stability. By following either of two strategies, the government can indeed stop this vicious circle, as has been demonstrated above. First, the government adopts tax finance of public interest while preserving full employment. And second, the government retires the residual of public debt at full employment.

Properly speaking, the government tries to reach two goals. On the one hand, it seeks to maintain full employment. On the other hand, it wishes to keep up long-run stability. In doing this, the government maximizes consumption (per head). As a result, there are many time paths of fiscal policy which achieve this. So the government may choose among them in a pragmatic manner. Anyhow, a necessary condition is that the budget must be balanced across the cycle.

In chapter 7, the analysis has been extended to include some further aspects. To begin with, in section 7.1., we dealt with the concept of full employment. Of course, the primary target of fiscal policy is to safeguard full employment. How should this notion be defined within the setting of a cyclical model? Does full employment prevail at the ceiling of the process or at its average? This issue is intimately connected with the objective of fiscal policy. The solution seems to be that the government should stabilize output at the average of the process. Only under these circumstances, the budget can be balanced over the cycle.

Then, in section 7.2., we discussed competing instruments to absorb an investment shock: Money finance of budget deficits, investment subsidies and monetary policy. How does monetary policy perform as compared to fiscal policy? Above all, monetary policy appears to be much more easy. In addition, it cures not the symptom but the cause. Government purchases, by way of contrast, immediately affect aggregate demand. Besides, we have to keep in mind that different institutions are concerned, the central bank and the government.

In the monograph, throughout, the focus was on an investment shock. As an exception to this rule, in section 7.3., we had a look at a monetary disturbance. In the first step, we outlined the ensuing process of adjustment. Then, in the second step, we explored to what extent fiscal and monetary policy are suited to overcome a monetary disturbance. Fiscal policy directly influences aggregate demand. In the long run, however, it drives output down to zero, hence the economy must collapse. As opposed to that, monetary policy quickly removes the cause of the disruption. Thus no difficulties are left.

So far, emphasis has been laid on a stationary economy. Now, in section 7.4., we addressed a growing economy. Imagine that the government, starting from a balanced budget, cuts the tax rate forever. Then, in the long run, public debt tends to explode, which squeezes private capital down to zero. As a consequence, there will be fatal crowding out. This finding agrees with the conclusions drawn for a stationary economy.

In the last step, we derived the optimum of fiscal policy. It proves useful to distinguish between two cases, depending on the private saving ratio. If private savings are high, the government should run a budget deficit over the cycle as a whole, thereby curbing private investment. Conversely, if private savings are low, the government ought to strive for a budget surplus across the cycle, thus stimulating capital formation. This outcome is in clear contrast to the results obtained for a stationary economy.

9. Result

Essentially, the analysis has been performed within an extended multiplier-accelerator model of a stationary economy. The focus was on the time path induced by an investment shock and, as a response, corrected by active fiscal policy.

In principle, the process of adjustment can be divided into two phases. At the beginning, the economy is in the long-run equilibrium. Particularly, all workers have got a job. Firms do not invest, so the stock of capital does not change. The budget balances, and there is no public debt.

In the first phase, sales expectations deteriorate exogenously. For that reason, businesses defer the replacement of capital. Private investment becomes negative, hence the stock of capital declines. In order to prevent unemployment from coming into existence, the government answers by a fiscal expansion. Properly speaking, the government increases public consumption. This brings the budget into deficit, giving rise to public debt.

In the second phase, sales expectations recover endogenously. Enterprises make up for the replacement of capital. Private investment turns positive, thereby replenishing the stock of capital. To avoid overemployment, the government switches over to a fiscal contraction. More precisely, the government reduces public consumption. Accordingly, the budget moves into surplus, thus retiring public debt.

In the long run, however, the economy enters a vicious circle where the government borrows in order to finance the interest payments on public debt. As a consequence, public debt tends to explode, which drives the stock of capital down to zero. That means, there will be fatal crowding out.

In summary, the investment shock generates a cyclical process of adjustment. This, in turn, requires a cyclical path of fiscal policy. In spite of that, the budget does not balance over the cycle as a whole. As a fundamental result, the long-run equilibrium proves to be unstable. Ultimately, the economy must break down.

This raises the question, whether the government can restore stability. Put another way, can the government stop the vicious circle? In discussing this problem, two strategies turn out to be fruitful. First, the government adopts tax finance of public interest at full employment. And second, the government pays off the residual of public debt at full employment.

Basically, fiscal policy serves two purposes. On the one hand, the government seeks to maintain full employment. On the other hand, the government wishes to keep up long-run stability. In doing this, the government maximizes consumption (per head). To conclude, there are many time paths of fiscal policy which achieve this. So the government may choose among them in a pragmatic manner. In any chase, a necessary condition is that the budget must be balanced over the cycle.

List of Symbols

A	reduced discriminant
B	budget deficit, public borrowing (real)
C	private consumption (real)
D	public debt (real)
E	expected sales (real)
F	labour market friction
G	public consumption, government purchases (real)
H	primary budget deficit (real)
I	private investment (real)
K	capital stock (real)
L	money demand (real)
M	money stock (nominal)
N	labour demand
$\bar{N}$	labour supply
P	price level
R	public interest payments (real)
S	private savings (of the young) (real)
T	income tax (real)
U	Lagrange function
Y	output, income (real)
Z	aggregate demand (real)
a	labour-output ratio
b	interest sensitivity of private investment, public borrowing ratio
c	marginal propensity to consume, private consumption per head
d	debt-capital ratio
f	per capita production function
g	public consumption ratio
h	interest sensitivity of money demand, primary deficit ratio
i	interest rate
k	income sensitivity of money demand, capital per head
n	growth rate of labour (population)
s	private savings per head, private saving ratio
t	tax rate
u	utility, unemployment rate
v	capital-output ratio
w	wage rate
y	output per head
z	markup rate, consumption per head
α	production function
β	production function
γ	utility function

δ	utility function
ε	utility function
η	interest elasticity of money demand
λ	speed of adjustment
μ	Lagrange multiplier
τ	time
¶	profits

References

Abel, A. B., An Analysis of Fiscal Policy under Operative and Inoperative Bequest Motives, in: E. Helpman, A. Razin, E. Sadka, Eds., Economic Effects of the Government Budget, Cambridge 1988.

Allen, P. R., Financing Budget Deficits, in: European Economic Review 10, 1977, 345-373.

Allen, R. G. D., Macroeconomic Theory, London 1967.

Andel, N., Finanzwissenschaft, Tübingen 1983.

Arrow, K. J., *Boskin*, M. J., Eds., The Economics of Public Debt, New York 1988.

Arrow, K. J., Kurz, M. Public Investment, the Rate of Return, and Optimal Fiscal Policy, Baltimore 1970.

Artis, M., Recent Developments in the Theory of Fiscal Policy, in: S. T. Cook, P. M. Jackson, Eds., Current Issues in Fiscal Policy, Oxford 1979.

Asada, T., Government Finance and Wealth Effect in a Kaldorian Cycle Model, in: Journal of Economics 47, 1987, 143-166.

Aschinger, G., Probleme der Staatsverschuldung, in: Jahrbücher für Nationalökonomie und Statistik 200, 1985, 582-601.

Assenmacher, W., Lehrbuch der Konjunkturtheorie, München 1987.

Atkinson, A. B., *Stiglitz*, J. E., Lectures on Public Economics, London 1980.

Auerbach, A. J., *Feldstein*, M., Eds., Handbook of Public Economics, Amsterdam 1987.

Auerbach, A. J., *Kotlikoff*, L. J., Dynamic Fiscal Policy, Cambridge 1987.

Bailey, M. J., The Optimal Full-Employment Surplus, in: Journal of Political Economy 80, 1972, 649-661.

Baltensperger, E., Government Expenditure Policies in Equilibrium and Disequilibrium, in: Kyklos 30, 1977, 421-442.

Barro, R. J., Are Government Bonds Net Wealth? in: Journal of Political Economy 82, 1974, 1095-1117.

Barro, R. J., Macroeconomics, New York, 1987.

Barro, R. J., Ed., Modern Business Cycle Theory, Cambridge 1989.

Barro, R. J., The Neoclassical Approach to Fiscal Policy, in: R. J. Barro, Ed., Modern Business Cycle Theory, Cambridge 1989.

Barro, R. J., The Ricardian Approach to Budget Deficits, in: Journal of Economic Perspectives 3, 1989, 37-54.

Barth, J. R., *Iden,* G. R., *Russek,* F. S., The Economic Consequences of Federal Deficits, in: Southern Economic Journal 52, 1986, 27-50.

Bartsch, P., Zur Theorie der längerfristigen Wirkungen „expansiver" Fiskalpolitik, Frankfurt 1986.

Beare, J. B., *Thakkar,* R. B., Optimal Government Bond Finance, in: Journal of Macroeconomics 10, 1988, 217-229.

Bender, D., u. a., Hg., Vahlens Kompendium der Wirtschaftstheorie und Wirtschaftspolitik, München 1988.

Benninga, S., *Protopapadakis,* A., The Neutrality of the Real Equilibrium under Alternative Financing of Government Expenditures, in: Journal of Monetary Economics 14, 1984, 183-208.

Bental, B., *Eckstein,* Z., Inflation, Deficit and Seignorage with Expected Stabilization, in: E. Helpman, A. Razin, E. Sadka, Eds., Economic Effects of the Government Budget, Cambridge 1988.

Bernheim, B. D., A Neoclassical Perspective on Budget Deficits, in: Journal of Economic Perspectives 3, 1989, 55-72.

Blanchard, O. J., Current and Anticipated Deficits, Interest Rates and Economic Activity, in: European Economic Review 25, 1984, 7-27.

Blanchard, O. J., Debt, Deficits, and Finite Horizons, in: Journal of Political Economy 93, 1985, 223-247.

Blanchard, O. J., *Fischer,* S., Lectures on Macroeconomics, Cambridge 1989.

Blinder, A. S., *Solow,* R. M., Analytical Foundations of Fiscal Policy, in: A. S. Blinder, R. M. Solow, Eds., The Economics of Public Finance, Washington 1974.

Blinder, A. S., *Solow,* R. M., Does Fiscal Policy Matter?, in: Journal of Public Economics 2, 1973, 319-337.

Blinder, A. S., *Solow,* R. M., Does Fiscal Policy Matter? A Correction, in: Journal of Public Economics 5, 1976, 183-184.

Blinder, A. S., *Solow,* R. M., Does Fiscal Policy Still Matter? A Reply, in: Journal of Monetary Economics 2, 1976, 501-510.

Blinder, A. S., *Solow,* R. M., Eds, The Economics of Public Finance, Washington 1974.

Böhm, V., Disequilibrium and Macroeconomics, Oxford 1989.

Bombach, G., *Gahlen,* B., *Ott,* A. E., Hg., Perspektiven der Konjunkturforschung, Tübingen 1984.

Boskin, M. J., Ed., Private Saving and Public Debt, Oxford 1987.

Brainard, W. C., *Tobin,* J., Pitfalls in Financial Model Building, in: American Economic Review, Papers and Proceedings 58, 1968, 99-122.

Branson, W. H., The Dual Roles of the Government Budget and the Balance of Payments in the Movement from Short-Run to Long-Run Equilibrium, in: Quarterly Journal of Economics 90, 1976, 345-367.

Brems, H., Fiscal Theory, Lexington 1983.

Brümmerhoff, D., Finanzwissenschaft, München 1989.

Brunner, K., *Meltzer,* A. H., An Aggregative Theory for a Closed Economy, in: J. Stein, Ed., Monetarism, Amsterdam 1976.

Brunner, K., *Meltzer,* A. H., Monetary Economics, New York 1989.

Bryant, J., Government Irrelevance Results: A Simple Exposition, in: American Economic Review 73, 1983, 758-761.

Buchanan, J. M., *Wagner,* R. E., Democracy in Deficit, New York 1977.

Buiter, W. H., Budgetary Policy, International and Intertemporal Trade in the Global Economy, Amsterdam 1989.

Buiter, W. H., A Guide to Public Sector Debt and Deficits, in: Economic Policy 1, 1985, 13-79.

Buiter, W. H., Temporary Equilibrium and Long-Run Equilibrium, New York 1979.

Burbidge, J. B., Government Debt in an Overlapping Generations Model with Bequests and Gifts, in: American Economic Review 73, 1983, 222-227.

Butkiewicz, J. L., On Fiscal Policy and Macroeconomic Stability, in: Public Finance Quarterly 10, 1982, 39-47.

Butkiewicz, J. L., The Impact of Debt Finance on Aggregate Demand, in: Journal of Macroeconomics 3, 1981, 77-90.

Caesar, R., Crowding-Out in der Bundesrepublik Deutschland, in: Kredit und Kapital 18, 1985, 265-276.

Calvo, G. A., *Obstfeld,* M., Optimal Time-Consistent Fiscal Policy with Finite Lifetimes: Analysis and Extensions, in: E. Helpman, A. Razin, E. Sadka, Eds., Economic Effects of the Government Budget, Cambridge 1988.

Cansier, D., Vermögenseffekte der Staatsverschuldung, in: Kredit und Kapital 14, 1981, 390-411.

Cansier, D., *Kath,* D., Hg., Öffentliche Finanzen, Kredit und Kapital, Berlin 1985.

Carlberg, M., Is Deficit Spending Feasible in the Long Run?, in: Zeitschrift für Wirtschafts- und Sozialwissenschaften 103, 1983, 409-418.

Carlberg, M., Makroökonomik der offenen Wirtschaft, München 1989.

Carlberg, M., Public Debt, Taxation and Government Expenditures in a Growing Economy, Berlin 1988.

Carlberg, M., Theorie der Arbeitslosigkeit, München 1988.

Carmichael, J., The Role of Government Financial Policy in Economic Growth, Unpublished Dissertation, Princeton University 1979.

Cassel, D., *Thieme,* H. J., Stabilitätspolitik, in: D. Bender u.a., Hg., Vahlens Kompendium, München 1988.

Cavaco-Silva, A. A., Economic Effects of Public Debt, London 1977.

Cebula, R. J., IS-LM Stability and Economic Policy Effectiveness, in: Journal of Macroeconomics 2, 1980, 181-183.

Christ, C. F., On Fiscal and Monetary Policies and the Government Budget Restraint, in: American Economic Review 69, 1979, 526-538.

Christ, C. F., A Simple Macroeconomic Model with a Government Budget Restraint, in: Journal of Political Economy 76, 1968, 53-67.

Christofides, L. N., Are Government Expenditures Likely to Be Contractionary?, in: Public Finance 29, 1974, 392-399.

Claassen, E. M., Grundlagen der makroökonomischen Theorie, München 1980.

Cohen, D., *De Leeuw,* F., A Note on the Government Budget Restraint, in: Journal of Monetary Economics 6, 1980, 547-560.

Cook, S. T., *Jackson,* P. M., Current Issues in Fiscal Policy, Oxford 1979.

Currie, D. A., Optimal Stabilization Policies and the Government Budget Constraint, in: Economica 43, 1976, 159-167.

Currie, D. A., *Gazioglou,* S., Wealth Effects, Treasury Bill Financing and Stability, in: Journal of Public Economics 21, 1983, 397-403.

Diamond, P. A., National Debt in a Neoclassical Growth Model, in: American Economic Review 55, 1965, 1126-1150.

Dieckheuer, G., Staatsverschuldung und wirtschaftliche Stabilisierung, Baden-Baden 1978.

Domar, E. D., The "Burden of the Debt" and the National Income, in: American Economic Review 34, 1944, 798-827.

Dornbusch, R., Comments on Brunner and Meltzer, in: J. L. Stein, Ed., Monetarism, Amsterdam 1976.

Dornbusch, R., Dollars, Debts and Deficits, Cambridge 1986.

Dornbusch, R., *Fischer,* S., Macroeconomics, New York 1987.

Drabicki, J. Z., *Takayama,* A., Money, National Debt, and Economic Growth, in: Journal of Economic Theory 33, 1984, 356-367.

Duguay, P., *Rabeau,* Y., A Simulation Model of Macroeconomic Effects of Deficit, in: Journal of Macroeconomics 10, 1988, 539-564.

Duwendag, D., Staatsverschuldung — Notwendigkeit und Gefahren, Baden-Baden 1983.

Eisner, R., Budget Deficits: Rhetoric and Reality, in: Journal of Economic Perspectives 3, 1989, 73-93.

Eisner, R., How Real is the Federal Deficit?, New York 1986.

Felderer, B., *Homburg,* S., Makroökonomik und neue Makroökonomik, Berlin 1989.

Feldstein, M., Debt and Taxes in the Theory of Public Finance, in: Journal of Public Economics 28, 1985, 233-245.

Feldstein, M., The Effects of Fiscal Policies When Incomes Are Uncertain: A Contradiction to Ricardian Equivalence, in: American Economic Review 78, 1988, 14-23.

Feldstein, M., Fiscal Policies, Inflation, and Capital Accumulation, in: American Economic Review 70, 1980, 636-650.

Fischer, S., Recent Developments in Macroeconomics, in: Economic Journal 98, 1988, 294-339.

Flaschel, P., *Krüger,* M., Eds., Recent Approaches to Economic Dynamics, Frankfurt 1988.

Flemming, J. S., Debt and Taxes in War and Peace: The Case of a Small Open Economy, in: M. J. Boskin, Ed., Private Saving and Public Debt, Oxford 1987.

Flemming, J. S., Debt and Taxes in War and Peace: The Closed Economy Case, in: K. J. Arrow, M. J. Boskin, Eds., The Economics of Public Debt, New York, 1988.

Foley, D. K., *Sidrauski,* M., Monetary and Fiscal Policy in a Growing Economy, London 1971.

Folkers, C., Begrenzungen von Steuern und Staatsausgaben in den USA, Baden-Baden 1983.

Francke, H. H., Portfolioeffekte öffentlicher Kreditnahme, Berlin 1981.

Francke, H. H., *Friedrich,* D., Zinswirkungen der Staatsverschuldung. Eine empirische Untersuchung für die Bundesrepublik Deutschland, Berlin 1984.

Franz, W., *Gaab,* W., Hg., Theoretische und angewandte Wirtschaftsforschung, Berlin 1988.

Frenkel, J. A., *Razin,* A., Fiscal Policies and the World Economy, Cambridge 1987.

Friedman, B. M., Day of Reckoning, New York 1988.

Friedman, B. M., *Hahn,* F. H., Eds., Handbook of Monetary Economics, Amsterdam 1990.

Friedman, M., A Monetary and Fiscal Framework for Economic Stability, in: American Economic Review 38, 1948, 245-264.

Fuhrmann, W., *Rohwedder,* J., Makroökonomik, München 1987.

von Furstenberg, G. M., Ed., The Government and Capital Formation, Cambridge, Mass. 1980.

Gabisch, G., *Lorenz,* H. W., Business Cycle Theory, Berlin 1989.

Gandenberger, O., Öffentliche Verschuldung II: Theoretische Grundlagen, in: W. Albers u.a., Hg., Handbuch der Wirtschaftswissenschaft, Stuttgart 1980.

Gandenberger, O., Theorie der öffentlichen Verschuldung, in: F. Neumark, Hg., Handbuch der Finanzwissenschaft, Tübingen 1981.

Gantner, M., Zur Frage nach den Grenzen der öffentlichen Verschuldung, in: E. Nowotny, Hg., Öffentliche Verschuldung, Stuttgart 1979.

Gebauer, W., Hg., Öffentliche Finanzen und monetäre Ökonomie, Frankfurt 1985.

Giavazzi, F., *Spaventa,* L., High Public Debt: The Italian Experience, Cambridge 1988.

Giersch, H., Konjunktur- und Wachstumspolitik in der offenen Wirtschaft, Wiesbaden 1977.

Goacher, D. J., National Savings, Fiscal Policy and Macroeconomic Stability, in: Oxford Economic Papers 36, 1984, 16-26.

Gorini, S., Debt, Wealth and the Rate of Growth: An Exercise in Equilibrium Dynamics, in: K. J. Arrow, M. J. Boskin, Eds., The Economics of Public Debt, New York 1988.

Gorini, S., The Neoclassical Theory of Public Debt and the Theory of a Long-Run Full-Employment Deficit, in: M. J. Boskin, Ed., Private Saving and Public Debt, Oxford 1987.

Gramlich, E. M., Budget Deficits and National Saving: Are Politicians Exogenous? in: Journal of Economic Perspectives 3, 1989, 23-35.

Grill, R., Der Staat im Modell optimalen Wachstums, Frankfurt 1989.

Gschwendtner, H., Fiskalpolitik und wirtschaftliche Stabilität, Tübingen 1980.

Gylfason, T., Fiscal Policy, Long-Run Stability and Aggregate Supply, in: European Economic Review 11, 1978, 99-103.

Hagemann, H., *Steiger,* O., Hg., Keynes' General Theory nach fünfzig Jahren, Berlin 1988.

Haller, H., Finanzwirtschaftliche Stabilisierungspolitik, in: F. Neumark, Hg., Handbuch der Finanzwissenschaft, Tübingen 1981.

Hamilton, J. D., *Flavin,* M. A., On the Limitations of Government Borrowing: A Framework for Empirical Testing, in: American Economic Review 76, 1986, 808-819.

Hansen, B., The Economic Theory of Fiscal Policy, London 1958.

Hansmeyer, K. H., Hg., Staatsfinanzierung im Wandel, Berlin 1983.

Hayakawa, H., Does Fiscal Policy Really Matter in the Context of Variable Prices?, in: Journal of Macroeconomics 1, 1979, 321-346.

Hedtkamp, G., Lehrbuch der Finanzwissenschaft, Neuwied 1977.

Helmstädter, E., Wirtschaftstheorie, Bd. 2, Makroökonomische Theorie, München 1986.

Helpman, E., *Razin,* A., *Sadka,* E., Eds., Economic Effects of the Government Budget, Cambridge 1988.

Helpman, E., *Sadka,* E., Optimal Financing of the Government's Budget: Taxes, Bonds, or Money?, in: American Economic Review 69, 1979, 152-160.

Hesse, H., Theoretische Grundlagen der "Fiscal Policy", München 1983.

Heubes, J., Finanztheorie, München 1985.

Heubes, J., Grundzüge der Konjunkturtheorie, München 1986.

Heubes, J., Makroökonomie, München 1982.

Hillier, B., Does Fiscal Policy Matter? in: Public Finance 32, 1977, 374-389.

Holmes, J. M., *Smyth,* D. J., Deficit Financing, Liquidity and the Government Budget Constraint, in: Journal of Macroeconomics 1, 1979, 83-106.

Ihori, T., Debt Burden and Intergeneration Equity, in: K. J. Arrow, M. J. Boskin, Eds., The Economics of Public Debt, New York 1988.

Ihori, T., Optimal Deficits in a Growing Economy, Discussion Paper 1988.

Infante, E. F., *Stein,* J. L., Does Fiscal Policy Matter?, in: Journal of Monetary Economics 2, 1976, 473-500.

Ip, P., Fiscal Policy and Stability in a Dynamic Macroeconomic Model with a Government Budget Constraint, in: Public Finance 32, 1977, 29-36.

Jäger, K., Diskrete und stetige Analyse im IS-LM Modell, in: Zeitschrift für die gesamte Staatswissenschaft 139, 1983, 229-244.

Jarchow, H. J., Theorie und Politik des Geldes, Göttingen 1988.

Johansen, L., Public Economics, Amsterdam 1965.

Karmann, A., *Ketterer*, K. H., Staatsverschuldung und Investitionstätigkeit, in: H. Göppl, R. Henn, Hg., Geld, Banken und Versicherungen, Karlsruhe 1981.

Kern, H., Monetäre Wirkungen der Staatsverschuldung, Berlin 1981.

Ketterer, K. H., Monetäre Aspekte der Staatsverschuldung, Berlin 1984.

Keynes, J. M., The General Theory of Employment, Interest and Money, London 1936.

Kitterer, W., Sind Steuern und Staatsverschuldung äquivalente Instrumente zur Finanzierung der Staatsausgaben?, in: Kredit und Kapital 19, 1986, 271-291.

Kitterer, W., Staatsverschuldung und intertemporale Allokation, in: Jahrbücher für Nationalökonomie und Statistik 204, 1988, 346-363.

Krause-Junk, G., Konsolidierung der öffentlichen Haushalte, strukturelles Defizit und konjunktureller Impuls, in: Finanzarchiv 40, 1982, 1-22.

Krause-Junk, G., Zur Relevanz des sogenannten strukturellen Defizits, in: Finanzarchiv 41, 1983, 52-59.

Krelle, W., Theorie des wirtschaftlichen Wachstums, Berlin 1988.

Kromphardt, J., Konjunkturtheorie heute: Ein Überblick, in: Zeitschrift für Wirtschafts- und Sozialwissenschaften 109, 1989, 173-231.

Lachmann, W., Fiskalpolitik, Berlin 1987.

Landmann, O., Die Stabilisierungspolitik im Spannungsfeld von Gleichgewichts- und Ungleichgewichtstheorie, in: Kyklos 35, 1982, 3-38.

Läufer, N. K. A., Fiskalpolitik versus Geldpolitik, in: Kredit und Kapital 8, 1975, 346-375.

Lehment, H., Fiskalpolitik in offenen Volkswirtschaften, Tübingen 1988.

Lucas, R. E., Models of Business Cycles, Oxford 1987.

Mackscheidt, K., *Steinhausen*, J., Finanzpolitik, Tübingen 1987.

Malinvaud, E., Mass Unemployment, Oxford 1984.

Malinvaud, E., Profitability and Unemployment, Cambridge 1980.

Malinvaud, E., The Theory of Unemployment Reconsidered, Oxford 1985.

Marini, G., *van der Ploeg*, F., Monetary and Fiscal Policy in an Optimising Model with Capital Accumulation and Finite Lives, in: Economic Journal 98, 1988, 772-786.

Masson, P. R., The Sustainability of Fiscal Deficits, in: IMF Staff Papers 32, 1985, 577-605.

Maußner, A., Stabilisierungspolitik im Lichte von Gleichgewichts- und Ungleichgewichtstheorie, Göttingen 1985.

Mayer, T., The Government Budget Constraint and Standard Macrotheory, in: Journal of Monetary Economics 13, 1984, 371-379.

McCallum, B. T., Are Bond-Financed Deficits Inflationary? in: Journal of Political Economy 92, 1984, 123-135.

McGrath, B., Implications of the Government Budget Constraint, in: Journal of Money, Credit and Banking 9, 1977, 304-315.

Meyer, L. H., The Economic Consequences of Government Deficits, Boston 1983.

Michaelis, J., Optimale Finanzpolitik im Modell überlappender Generationen, Frankfurt 1989.

Miller, S. M., Dynamic Monetary and Fiscal Policy and the Government Budget Restraint: A Growth Equilibrium, in: Journal of Macroeconomics 2, 1980, 199-212.

Mitchell, D. W., The Feasibility of Perpetual Deficits, in: Journal of Macroeconomics 10, 1988, 407-419.

Modigliani, F., The Debate Over Stabilization Policy, Cambridge 1986.

Modigliani, F., Long-Run Implications of Alternative Fiscal Policies and the Burden of the National Debt, in: Economic Journal 71, 1961, 730-755.

Modigliani, F., *Ando*, A., Impacts of Fiscal Actions on Aggregate Income and the Monetarist Controversy: Theory and Evidence, in: J. L. Stein, Ed., Monetarism, Amsterdam 1976.

Modigliani, F., *Sterling*, A., Government Debt, Government Spending, and Private Sector Behavior: Comment, in: American Economic Review 76, 1986, 1168-1179.

Monissen, H. G., Including a Government Budget Restraint in Standard Macroeconomic Analysis, in: Finanzarchiv 31, 1973, 193-223.

Mückl, W. J., Ein Beitrag zur Theorie der Staatsverschuldung, in: Finanzarchiv 39, 1981, 253-278.

Musgrave, R. A., *Musgrave*, B., Public Finance in Theory and Practice, New York 1989.

Nachtkamp, H. H., *Sinn*, H. W., Die konjunkturellen Wirkungen der Schuldenstrukturpolitik, in: Finanzarchiv 39, 1981, 279-305.

Nagatani, K., Macroeconomic Dynamics, Cambridge 1982.

Negishi, T., Microeconomic Foundations of Keynesian Macroeconomics, Amsterdam 1979.

Neumann, M., Theoretische Volkswirtschaftslehre, München 1988.

Neumann, M. J. M., Inflation und Staatsverschuldung, in: Zeitschrift für Wirtschafts- und Sozialwissenschaften 101, 1981, 113-126.

Niehans, J., The Theory of Money, Baltimore 1978.

Nowotny, E., Der öffentliche Sektor, Berlin 1987.

Nowotny, E., Hg., Öffentliche Verschuldung, Stuttgart 1979.

Oates, W. E., Budget Balance and Equilibrium Income, in: Journal of Finance 21, 1966, 489-498.

O'Connell, S. A. O., *Zeldes*, S. P., Rational Ponzi Games, in: International Economic Review 29, 1988, 431-450.

O'Driscoll, G. P., Jr., The Ricardian Nonequivalence Theorem, in: Journal of Political Economy 85, 1977, 207-210.

Ohr, R., Budgetpolitik in offenen Volkswirtschaften, Berlin 1987.

Okun, A., Prices and Quantities, Oxford 1981.

Ott, D. J., *Ott*, A. F., Budget Balance and Equilibrium Income, in: Journal of Finance 20, 1965, 71-77.

Patinkin, D., Money, Interest and Prices, New York 1965.

Peacock, A., *Shaw*, G. K., The Economic Theory of Fiscal Policy, London 1982.

Peffekoven, R., Öffentliche Finanzen, in: D. Bender u. a., Hg., Vahlens Kompendium der Wirtschaftstheorie und Wirtschaftspolitik, München 1988.

Penner, R. G., Government Deficits: The Case of the United States, in: M. J. Boskin, Ed., Private Saving and Public Debt, Oxford 1987.

Persson, T., *Svensson*, L. E. O., Checks and Balances on the Government Budget, in: E. Helpman et al., Eds., Economic Effects of the Government Budget, Cambridge 1988.

Pestieau, P., *Possen*, U. M., Optimal Growth and Distribution Policies, in: Journal of Public Economics 9, 1978, 357-372.

Petersen, H. G., Finanzwissenschaft, Stuttgart 1988.

Pfähler, W., Kurz-, mittel- und langfristige Effekte der Fiskalpolitik in diskreter Analyse, in: Finanzarchiv 40, 1982, 281-305.

Phelps, E. S., *Shell*, K., Public Debt, Taxation and Capital Intensiveness, in: Journal of Economic Theory 1, 1969, 330-346.

Phelps, E. S., *Velupillai*, K., Optimum Fiscal Policy when Monetary Policy is Bound by a Rule: Ramsey Redux, in: K. J. Arrow, M. J. Boskin, Eds., The Economics of Public Debt, New York 1988.

Phillips, A. W., Stabilisation Policy in a Closed Economy, in: Economic Journal 64, 1954, 290-323.

Pohl, R., Theorie der Inflation, München 1981.

Pohmer, D., Finanzwissenschaft III: Politik, in: W. Albers u. a., Hg., Handwörterbuch der Wirtschaftswissenschaft, Stuttgart 1981.

Pohmer, D., Wirkungen finanzpolitischer Instrumente, in: F. Neumark, Hg., Handbuch der Finanzwissenschaft, Tübingen 1977.

Possen, U. M., The Long-Run Properties of an Income-Expenditure Model, Economica 46, 1979, 159-173.

Possen, U. M., A Study of an Income Expenditure Model, in: Quarterly Journal of Economics 88, 1974, 434-453.

Pui, C. U., Fiscal Policy and Stability in a Dynamic Macroeconomic Model with a Government Budget Restraint, in: Public Finance 32, 1977, 29-36.

Ramser, H. J., Beschäftigung und Konjunktur, Berlin 1987.

Rau, N., Simplifying the Theory of the Government Budget Restraint, in: Oxford Economic Papers 37, 1985, 210-229.

Reither, F., Kapitalstock, Staatsverschuldung und rationale Erwartungen, Hamburg 1988.

Richter, R., Geldtheorie, Berlin 1987.

Rose, M., Finanzwissenschaftliche Makrotheorie, München 1980.

Rose, M., Lerners funktionale Finanzpolitik — einige Konsequenzen für die Makropolitik, in: Finanzarchiv 46, 1988, 351-367.

Samuelson, P. A., An Exact Consumption-Loan Model of Interest With or Without the Social Contrivance of Money, in: Journal of Political Economy 66, 1958, 467-482.

Samuelson, P. A., Interactions Between the Multiplier Analysis and the Principle of Acceleration, in: Review of Economics and Statistics 21, 1939, 75-78.

Samuelson, P. A., Principles and Rules in Modern Fiscal Policy: A Neo-Classical Reformulation, in: Money, Trade and Economic Growth, New York 1955.

Samuelson, P. A., *Nordhaus*, W. D., Economics, New York 1989.

Sargent, T. J., Macroeconomic Theory, Boston 1987.

Sargent, T. J., *Wallace*, N., Some Unpleasant Monetarist Arithmetic, in: Federal Reserve Board of Minneapolis Quarterly Review 5, 1981, 1-17.

Scarth, W. M., Bond-Financed Fiscal Policy and the Problem of Instrument Instability, in: Journal of Macroeconomics 1, 1979, 107-117.

Scarth, W. M., A Note on the "Crowding Out" of Private Expenditures by Bond Financed Increases in Government Spending, in: Journal of Public Economics 5, 1976, 385-387.

Scheele, E., Vermögensrestriktion, Budgetrestriktionen, Wirkungen der Staatsverschuldung und die Budgetmultiplikatoren von Dieter Cansier, in: Kredit und Kapital 16, 1983, 36-53.

Schlieper, U., Staatsverschuldung im langfristigen Gleichgewicht, in: H. Siebert, Hg., Intertemporale Allokation, Frankfurt 1984.

Schmid, M., Fiscal Ponzi Games in a World Economy, in: H. Schneider, H. Herberg, F. Gehrels, Hg., Inflation und Beschäftigung in offenen Volkswirtschaften, Berlin 1989.

Schmid, M., Fiscal Strategies, Foreign Indebtedness, and Overlapping Generations, in: Empirica, 1988, 95-115.

Schmidt, K., Öffentliche Verschuldung, in: W. Albers, Hg., Handwörterbuch der Wirtschaftswissenschaft, Stuttgart 1980.

Schneider, H., *Herberg*, H., Gehrels, F., Hg., Inflation und Beschäftigung in offenen Volkswirtschaften, Berlin 1989.

Seidmann, L. S., The Government Deficit in a Growth Model, in: Journal of Macroeconomics 9, 1987, 593-611.

Shieh, Y. N., The Efficacy of Bond-Financed Fiscal Policy, in: Public Finance Quarterly 10, 1982, 119-125.

Siebert, H., Intertemporale Allokation, Frankfurt 1984.

Siebke, J., *Knoll,* D., *Schmidberger,* W. D., Theoretische Grundlagen des crowding-out-Effektes, in: W. Ehrlicher, Hg., Geldpolitik, Zins und Staatsverschuldung, Berlin 1981.

Sinclair, P. J. N., Ed., Prices, Quantities and Expectations, Oxford 1987.

Sinn, H. W., Pro und contra Crowding-Out, in: Kredit und Kapital 16, 1983, 488-512.

Smith, G., A Dynamic IS-LM Simulation Model, in: Applied Economics 12, 1980, 313-327.

Smith, G., Flexible Policies and IS-LM Dynamics, in: Journal of Macroeconomics 4, 1982, 155-178.

Smith, G., The Long-Run Consequences of Monetary and Fiscal Policies when the Government Budget is Not Balanced, in: Journal of Public Economics 11, 1979, 59-79.

Smith, G., Monetarism, Bondism, and Inflation, in: Journal of Money, Credit and Banking 14, 1982, 278-286.

Smyth, D. J., Built-in-Flexibility of Taxation, the Government Budget Constraint, the Specification of the Demand for Money Function and the Stability of an IS-LM System, in: Public Finance 33, 1978, 367-375.

Smyth, D. J., Treasury Bill Financing in a Dynamic Macroeconomic Model with a Government Budget Restraint, in: Economic Letters 5, 1980, 225-229.

Solow, R. M., Growth Theory and After, in: American Economic Review 78, 1988, 307-317.

Spaventa, L., The Growth of Public Debt: Sustainability, Fiscal Rules, and Monetary Rules, in: IMF Staff Papers 34, 1987, 374-399.

Stein, J. L., Ed., Monetarism, Amsterdam 1976.

Stein, J. L., Monetarist, Keynesian and New Classical Economics, New York 1982.

Steindl, F. G., A Simple Macroeconomic Model with a Government Budget Restraint: A Comment, in: Journal of Political Economy 79, 1971, 675-679.

Stiglitz, J. E., On the Relevance or Irrelevance of Public Financial Policy, in: K. J. Arrow, M. J. Boskin, Eds., The Economics of Public Debt, New York 1988.

Tanzi, V., *Bleijer,* M. I., Public Debt and Fiscal Policy in Developing Countries, in: K. J. Arrow, M. J. Boskin, Eds., The Economics of Public Debt, New York 1988.

Tichy, G., Konjunkturpolitik, Berlin 1988.

Tobin, J., Asset Accumulation and Economic Activity, Oxford 1980.

Tobin, J., The Monetary-Fiscal Mix: Long-Run Implications, in: American Economic Association, Papers and Proceedings 76, 1986, 213-218.

Tobin, J., *Buiter,* W. H., Long-Run Effects of Fiscal and Monetary Policy on Aggregate Demand, in: J. L. Stein, Ed., Monetarism, Amsterdam 1976.

Tolkemitt, G., Zur Theorie der langfristigen Wirkungen öffentlicher Verschuldung, Tübingen 1975.

Turnovsky, S. J., Monetary and Fiscal Policy in a Long-Run Macroeconomic Model, in: Economic Record 56, 1980, 158-170.

Vogt, W., Eine Verallgemeinerung der Wachstumstheorie, in: Weltwirtschaftliches Archiv 92, 1964, 259-296.

Vosgerau, H. J., Konjunkturtheorie, in: W. Albers u.a., Hg., Handwörterbuch der Wirtschaftswissenschaft, Stuttgart 1978.

Wang, L. F. S., IS-LM Stability and Economic Policy Effectiveness: A Note, in: Journal of Macroeconomics 2, 1980, 175-179.

Weil, P., Permanent Budget Deficits and Inflation, in: Journal of Monetary Economics 20, 1987, 393-410.

Weitzman, M. L., The Simple Macroeconomics of Profit Sharing, in: American Economic Review 75, 1985, 937-953.

von *Weizsäcker*, C. C., Das eherne Zinsgesetz, in: Kyklos 32, 1979, 270-282.

Wenig, A., Konjunkturtheorie, in: R. Selten, Hg., Handwörterbuch der Mathematischen Wirtschaftswissenschaften, Wiesbaden 1979.

Wenzel, H. D., Defizitfinanzierung als Instrument einer zielorientierten Finanzpolitik, Baden-Baden 1983.

Westphal, U., Makroökonomik, Berlin 1988.

Whitmore, H. W., Unbalanced Government Budgets, Private Asset Holdings, and the Traditional Comparative Static Multipliers, in: Journal of Macroeconomics 2, 1980, 129-157.

van *Wijnbergen*, S., Inflation, Balance of Payments Crises, and Public Sector Deficits, in: E. Helpman et al., Eds., Economic Effects of the Government Budget, Cambridge 1988.

Wolfstetter, E., Fiscal Policy and the Classical Growth Cycle, in: Zeitschrift für Nationalökonomie 42, 1982, 375-393.

Yellen, J. L., Symposium on the Budget Deficit, in: Journal of Economic Perspectives 3, 1989, 17-21.

Zimmermann, H., *Henke*, K. D., Finanzwissenschaft, München 1987.

Index

MIX
Papier aus verantwortungsvollen Quellen
Paper from responsible sources
FSC® C105338

Printed by Libri Plureos GmbH
in Hamburg, Germany